The Harmonization of Working Life and Family Life

The Harmonization of Working Life and Family Life

Bulletin of Comparative Labour Relations 30 - 1995

Editor: R. Blanpain
Guest Editors: K. Sugeno & Y. Suwa

Contributors:

J. Bellace
M. Biagi
C. Engels
J.-Cl. Javillier
M. Kurokawa
A. Neal
A. Numhauser-Henning

1995
Kluwer Law International
The Hague / London / Boston

Kluwer Law International

P.O. Box 85889
2508 CN The Hague
The Netherlands

Tel.: 31-70-3081500
Fax: 31-70-3081515

Distribution in the USA and Canada:

Massachusetts Avenue
Cambridge, MA 02139
USA

Tel.: 1-617-354-00140
Fax: 1-617-354-8595

A C.I.P. Catalogue record for this book is available from the Library of Congress

ISBN 90411-0064-4

Table of Contents

Note on Guest Editors

Kazuo Sugeno graduated from the University of Tokyo, Faculty of Law in 1966. His major publications include INDUSTRIAL ACTIONS AND DAMAGES (The Tokyo University, 1978) and JAPANESE LABOR LAW (The University of Washington Press, 1992). He is currently a professor of law at the University of Tokyo Faculty of Law.

Yasuo Suwa graduated from Hitotsubashi University, Faculty of Law in 1970. He went on to graduate from the University of Tokyo Graduate School of Law and Politics in 1977. His major publications include SETTLEMENT OF LABOR DISPUTES (Nihon Roshikankei Kyokai, 1991) and EMPLOYMENT RELATIONS LAW (with K. Sugeno, Sogo-Rodo-Kenkyujo, 1994). He is currently a professor of law at Hosei University Faculty of Sociology.

Preface

The papers published in this volume of the Bulletin are the result of a seminar sponsored by the Japanese Institute of Labour, which was held in Tokyo, Japan on September 24, 1994 under the guidance and scientific direction of Professors Kazuo Sugeno and Yasuo Suwa of the University of Tokyo. The seminar culminated in a fascinating all-day discussion of this very important and complex topic.

The issue of harmonizing working life and family life is one which has recently come to the forefront of labour relations in many countries around the world. Probably the most significant single factor to explain this evolution is the dramatic increase of women in the workforce since the 1960's. As women continue to work and achieve higher status in the workforce, these issues will remain salient. And why should it be that the issue of harmonizing working and family life depends so much on the presence of women in the workforce? Because the reality has been that family responsibilities fall disproportionately upon women and they must now try to juggle more professional responsibilities with their family responsibilities.

The papers in this edition of the Bulletin come from countries which perhaps diverge the greatest among each other as far as their approaches to these issues. On one end of the spectrum is the United States of America, where the legislative and executive bodies are still debating paid maternity leave and on the other end of the spectrum is Sweden, where this is an issue long decided upon.

Workers and unions are able to take advantage of such measures as working time flexibility, reduction of working hours, parental leave, maternity leave with the right to a guaranteed job upon return to the workplace, child benefits, and provisions for child care. These measures are a few of those discussed by most of the reports presented here. The reader will be keen to note that such measures have not always come about with the specific intention of harmonizing family and work life. In several cases, this has been a beneficial fortuity. The reader will also notice a great divergence in the level of development in approaching these issues: Some countries are just beginning to tackle these issues, while for others they may be the hallmark of their labour relations system.

The hope is, as always, that this Bulletin will be a catalyst for further study and discussion on this important topic. A greater balance between work and family responsibilities can be achieved through developing measures to facilitate working and family life, with workers and their families being the worthy beneficiaries. Thanks goes to Takashi Araki, Ryuichi Yamakawa, Chris Engels, Lisa Salas and the Japanese Institute of Labour for their assistance in realizing this volume of the Bulletin.

Belgium

Chris Engels

INTRODUCTION

While the question of how to combine and harmonize working life and family life is, on the face of it, a sex neutral question, it is one that is often asked by an ever increasing part of the female population that is entering the labor market.

In the 20-year period between 1970 and 1990, female employment in Belgium rose from 1,200,000 workers to 1,700,000 workers. In the period 1991–1992, male employment decreased by about 25,000 workers, while female employment rose by 7,000 jobs.

One could question whether legal provisions guaranteeing equality of treatment are sufficient to allow these women to participate in working life on a really equal footing with men.

Looking at the question from a different angle, can employees who are participating in working life on a full-time basis actually modify their working patterns in order to adapt to an increasingly important role in family life?

I. EQUAL EMPLOYMENT LEGISLATION IN GENERAL – ITS INSUFFICIENCY IN CREATING TRULY EQUAL OPPORTUNITIES

Belgian equal employment legislation came into being because of European Community incentives. The Parliamentary Act of 4 August 1978, referred to as the Economic Reform Act, is the center piece of Belgian equal employment opportunity legislation. It deals with equality of treatment between men and women relating to conditions of employment and access to employment, vocational training, promotion and self-employment opportunities. (Title V, Economic Reform Act, 4 August 1978; See: Blanpain, R. and Engels, C., Belgium, in *Int'l Ency. Lab. L. & Indus. Rel.*, Kluwer, Deventer, s.d., 57–60) The Act covers both the public and the private sector. Its provisions are mandatory. Any contrary contract stipulation, whether in a collective bargaining agreement or in an individual contract of employment will be null and void.

Article 118 of the Act defines unequal treatment as any form of discrimination on the grounds of sex, either directly, or indirectly by referring to the marital status or the family situation. Since indirect discrimination is also prohibited, the actual intention of the employer is of lesser importance. The Act concentrates on the consequences of the employer's action. Equality of treatment is aimed at and this during the various stages of an employment relationship. Equality of treatment is the rule not only for access to employment, but also with regard to promotions and other conditions of employment.

The Economic Reform Act states a number of exceptions to the stringent

rules prohibiting discrimination on the basis of sex:
- protection of motherhood, including both maternity and pregnancy (see *infra*);
- positive actions (see *infra*);
- the determination of *bona fide* occupational qualifications for which by reason of the nature of the job or the conditions in which the job is carried out, the sex of the worker concerned is considered to be a determining factor;
- underground labor in mines and
- the presently very controversial issue of night work (see *infra*).

The Economic Reform Act incorporates penal sanctions for its violations. Furthermore, contractual stipulations and practices contrary to the provisions and rules contained in the Act are null and void. Any prejudiced person can bring an action for enforcement in court. Trade unions are granted the right to sue in all litigation arising out of the application of the Act and in defence of their members' rights. Since Belgian trade unions do not have legal personality, an explicit statutory provision to that extent was necessary.

The court can order an employer to cease engaging in discriminatory practices relating to vocational training, working conditions or criteria for dismissal. Penal sanctions can be applied in case of non-observance of the court order. The protection of employees who filed complaints based on the Act is equally provided in the Economic Reform Act. For example, if an employee is fired after lodging a complaint, the burden of proof will rest upon the employer to prove that lodging the complaints had nothing to do with that particular worker getting fired. If the employer is not able to rebut the inferences of discrimination it has an option either of reinstating the employee, or paying an additional lump sum payment of six months of wages.

The reversal of the burden of proof is only installed in cases of alleged retaliation and not for any other violation of the Act. Ordinary violations are not sanctioned through a lump sum indemnity. Both characteristics make the successful enforcement of equal employment opportunity legislation much harder. Issues dealing with the reversal of the burden of proof in discrimination cases remain under much debate, not only in Belgium, but also at the level of the European Union.

The provisions of the Economic Reform Act are an important step towards the realization of equal opportunities for both sexes. However, its actual scope is rather restricted. It does not provide a guarantee of access to employment. The Economic Reform Act is not aimed at creating a balanced work force. In practice one has to observe that almost 20 years after passing the Act, not many law suits are based on it, even though when reading the Act one would think it to have 'sufficient bite.' Employees who have been discriminated against have a hard time finding legal aid. Their trade unions, have up till now not been very instrumental in bringing cases before the courts. One could question whether their loyalty towards their male majority of members has anything to do with this. Also the powers of the courts are not sufficiently far reaching to have a real impact.

It is clear from the above that 'more' is needed in order to create real equality of opportunities for both male and female workers. Taking into account the fact that the burdens of family life have traditionally weighed more heavily on women then on men and have created actual impediments on true female participation at all levels of employment, it becomes clear that more is needed than a bare guarantee that terms and conditions of employment will not be differentiated on the basis of sex.

This last observation clarifies the perspective from which the present paper will continue to treat the subject: to what extent have measures been taken, either by the government, or by the social actors in order to create equality of outcome rather than equality of process? To express it differently, to what extent have measures been taken to allow women, and to a much smaller extent men, to fully participate in working life regardless of the normal family duties and obligations?

II. PROTECTION SPECIFICALLY AIMED AT PRODUCING CONDITIONS FOR PARTICIPATION IN EMPLOYMENT ON AN EQUAL BASIS

1. Pregnancy and Maternity Leave

A. Protection at the Hiring Stage

It is an established principle that an employee cannot be discriminated against because of her pregnancy. Some discussion arose in case law dealing with the question of whether a pregnant employee could be fired if she had not divulged the pregnancy to the employer when she applied for the job. Some courts considered the employee to have some form of information duty towards the employer. Not divulging information would then be considered fraud and could lead to dismissal for just cause.

However, if the pregnancy itself is legally protected, so should be be the information regarding it. If the information is not relevant for the job she applied for, the employee should be entitled to keep secret the pregnancy during the application procedures.

It should be mentioned here that the European Court of Justice considered pregnancy discrimination to be a direct form of discrimination. Justifying any distinction among employees on the basis of pregnancy, but not for the protection of pregnant women, will therefore become very hard. The European Court of Justice therefore took the realistic approach and refused to consider pregnancy discrimination as a form of indirect discrimination making a distinction between pregnant and non-pregnant persons, the way the American Supreme Court did some time ago. (See: Case No C-177/88, *Elisabeth Johanna Pacifica Dekker v. Stichting Vormingscentrum voor Jong Volwassenen (VJV-Centrum) Plus*, 8 November 1990, *Int'l Ency. Lab. L. & Indus. Rel.*, Kluwer, Deventer, Case law, Vol. 3, Case No 153.)

A refusal to hire a pregnant woman because of the additional costs involved in her employment would therefore run counter to directly applicable European Union provisions, in all of the European Union Member States, and would thus be unacceptable.

B. Working Conditions

Normal working conditions should apply to the pregnant woman. However, if she is employed in a job that could cause a danger to the health of the pregnant women or her fetus, she could be removed from the place of work. (See Labor Act, 16 March 1971, often amended afterwards, in *Int'l Ency. Lab. L. & Indus. Rel.*, Kluwer, Deventer, Vol. Legislation, Legislation Belgium, Act. n. 39, 143.)

In case the labor (or industrial) doctor prohibits her to do certain work, other work should be provided to her. If such an arrangement cannot be made she will have to interrupt working as long as the work could cause a danger to her health of the health of the fetus.

Similar provisions apply during the lactation period (up to 5 months after giving birth).

It is important to stress that the women concerned are entitled to sickness benefits for the period during which they cannot work for the above mentioned reasons. Even their entitlement to holiday pay is safeguarded during that time.

Pregnant women cannot be forced to perform overtime, even in these circumstances in which the employer could force the other employees to accept the overwork. Neither can they be forced to participate in flexible working time schemes (see *infra*).

During the last seven days preceding the estimated date of birth of the child the employee is not allowed to work any more. The same holds for an 8 week period following the date of birth of the child.

As soon as the period of pregnancy and maternity leave has come to an end, and the suspension of the performance of the contract of employment ends, the employee is entitled to be granted the same working conditions as before. It should not come as a surprise though that women often face practical problems getting back into the positions they were in before the pregnancy leave. In practice the pregnancy leave almost always seems to have some detrimental effect on the woman's career.

C. Protection against Dismissal

From the moment that the employee informs the employer of her pregnancy, she can no longer be fired for that reason. The employer is still able to fire the employee for any other reason unrelated to the pregnancy (as long as it does not violate another rule, of course). However, the burden of proof is upon the employer to establish that the reason for the termination is unrelated to the pregnancy.

The protection against dismissal remains into force until one month after the end of the pregnancy leave. If the employer terminates the contract of employment of the pregnant employee without being able to prove that the reason for the termination is unrelated to the pregnancy, the employer needs to pay the normal termination indemnity and a lump sum indemnity of three months of pay. Any notice that is given will only take effect after the pregnancy leave.

A parliamentary amendment has been recently introduced in order to enhance the protection that is granted to pregnant employees. The lump sum indemnity would, according to the proposal be doubled (six months).

D. Leave Granted

The performance of the contract of employment will be suspended during the absence of the pregnant employee giving birth and breast-feeding the child. The pregnant employee has a right to ask for leave of absence for a seven week period prior to the date at which she is supposed to give birth to the baby. The employee will give the employer a medical certificate indicating the estimated date of birth of her child. If it so happens that the baby is born at a later date, the period of leave will be prolonged till the day the baby was actually born.

The employee will be on mandatory leave at least 7 days prior to the estimated date of birth of the child and for an additional period of 8 weeks after confinement. Upon request of the employee this period will be prolonged with a period of leave the employee could have taken prior to giving birth but did not. The employee is entitled to take 7 weeks of leave before the estimated date of birth. One week is mandatory rest. It is thus possible that an employee who takes only 1 week before giving birth prolongs her leave up to 14 weeks in total, following the birth of the child.

If the baby has to stay in hospital (for at least 8 weeks) the continuance of the 8 week maternity leave can be postponed till the baby is allowed to leave the hospital.

As has already been mentioned, upon termination of the leave, the employee is entitled to be put back to work at the same conditions as before the leave took place.

E. Maternity Benefits – a True Equal Opportunity Amendment
Since 1990 the duty to pay the employee on pregnancy and maternity leave is no longer carried by the employer. Maternity pay will from now on be covered by medical insurance, as part of the social security system. The additional and direct costs involved in having female employees of child bearing age among the work force is thereby reduced. The remaining costs largely deal with replacing the employee on leave and training the replacing worker. However, the direct costs involved in paying guaranteed wages during leave is, so to say, 'socialized' and not to be borne by the single employer anymore. Indirect cost may still be borne by the employer, in as much as the employee may be incapacitated to work due to the pregnancy but not during the period of leave as described above. In that case the employer has to pay guaranteed wages in the same way as it would for any other sickness causing an incapacity to work.

In order to pay for the costs involved social security contributions are raised by 0.12%.

The level of benefits the employee on leave receives is:

- 82% of the salary she would receive if not on leave, and this during the first 30 days of her leave;
- 75% from the 31st day on, however, with a ceiling of around US$ 100 a day (as per 1 May 1994: 3,484.75-BF);
- if the leave continues beyond the 15 week period, 60% of pay.

At present a study is underway, in order to evaluate to what extent the Belgian legislation dealing with pregnancy and maternity protection is in conformity with the applicable European Union directive of 19 October 1992. Amendments will have to be implemented dealing with the evaluation of the risks to which the pregnant women is subject during employment. (See: Advice National Labor Relations Council, No 1,092, 29 March 1994.)

2. Paternity Leave and Parental Leave

Upon death or hospital confinement of the mother, the father-employee will be entitled to take paternity leave in order to take care of the baby.

A true form of parental leave – in the sense that the contract of employment of the father would also remain in existence during the time he is taking care of the child – did not exist however, until recently. A Royal Decree of 17 October 1994 brought about this change. The performance of the contract of employment of the father will be suspended during the father's paternity leave.

From the moment of notification of the paternity leave to the employer, the male employee cannot be fired, except for reasons unrelated to the paternity leave. If the contract of employment of the male employee is terminated during the paternity leave, the employer will carry the burden of proof and will have to establish that the termination is unrelated to the paterminty leave. The employee's protection ends when the paternity leave itself comes to an end.

The employer that terminated a male employee on paternity leave, who is not able to demonstrate that the employee was fired for reasons unrelated to the paternity leave, will have to pay a lump sum indemnity equal to three months of gross wages.

III. DIRECT EMPLOYMENT OPPORTUNITIES SHARED ON A MORE SEX-BLIND BASIS

The provisions discussed in this section are sex-blind, in as much as they offer opportunities regardless of the sex of the worker. Since these provisions increase flexibility, they could be used as tools to try to harmonize working life and family life. However, it should be stressed that the introduction of the rules discussed in the previous part of the paper was never as such aimed at the harmonization of working life and family life. If the rules can and are used to this purpose, this is merely a secondary effect.

The rules concerning the different forms of leave the employee can get and/or is entitled to are also sex-blind. However, they seem to be used more by women workers than by men. The rules discussed sub section 2 seem to grant some opportunities for the harmonization of working and family life.

1. Flexible Work Patterns

A. Part-Time Work

The concept of part-time work remains undefined in Belgian labor law. Specific legal measures – such as a Parliamentary Act and national collective bargaining agreements – have addressed the issue of part-time work, however.

Part-time work is dealt with by a Parliamentary Act of 22 December 1989, amending the Act concerning contracts of employment, and by an inter-industry wide collective bargaining agreement of 27 February 1981. Since part-time work has no specific legal definition, the concept has to be understood in contrast with the concept of full-time work. The hours of work, a full time worker would work are determined both by national legislation, and (primarily) by industry wide collective bargaining agreements. Somebody working less than full-time hours is considered to be a part-time worker. The minimum hours worked during any working period may not be less than 3 hours. Furthermore, legal provisions determine that weekly working time of the part-time worker may not be less than one-third of the weekly working time of the full-time worker with the same job qualification or of the weekly working time applicable in the same sector.

The contract of employment for part-time work needs to be in writing, and for each employee separately and prior to actually starting the performance.

Part-time workers should enjoy the same benefits as full-time workers, at least on a proportional basis. It should be stressed that any discrimination against part-time workers may result in a form of indirect sex-discrimination, since part-time work is still predominantly female.

Even though part-time work schedules are encouraged, all legal rules still take as a starting premise that full-time employment is the rule, and part-time employment, the exception. An expression of this preference is found in the rule that grants part-time workers priority for full-time jobs if they become available within the company and the employee desires to obtain that position.

As in most countries the increase in the active female participation in employment is combined with an increase in the rise of part-time work. One notices a difference in the age of women 'opting' for part time work. They are predominantly between the age of 25 and 45. A 1991 government report makes the connection with the fact that it is this category of workers that is taking care of the small children and is thus 'forced' into part-time employment.

One can also discover a correlation between the marital status of the female worker and the participation in part-time employment. While married women work part-time at a much higher rate than their male partners do, single women work part-time only to the same extent as their male colleagues. (See: Degimbe, N. and Simon, A., 'Vrouwenarbeid: Activiteitsgraad en deeltijdse arbeid', in *Arbeidsblad*, 1991, December issue, 12 *et seq.*) Statistics show that about 70% of women opt for part-time employment because they cannot find full-time employment. Even for those 30 years of age, 35% of the women indicated to be an involuntary part-time worker.

B. Temporary Work

Temporary work is strictly regulated under a Parliamentary Act of 24 July 1987. The concept of temporary work is strictly defined. Even though the use of temporary work is on the rise, it remains exceptional. The legal provisions determining when it is impossible to make use of temporary work make this easily understandable.

The law states that temporary work consists of:

a) the replacement of a permanent worker (e.g. in case of sickness, vacation, maternity leave);
b) help in case of an extraordinary increase in the work-load (due to e.g. a sudden increase in orders);
c) the fulfillment of exceptional work to be carried out (caused by an accident or the creation of a new department for which the employer has not yet been able to hire permanent employees).

C. Other Flexible Contracts

A. On Call Contract. Some companies, such as supermarkets, used 'on-call' contracts according to which the employee would have to work for an unspecified number of hours a week, for example in between 0 and 20 hours, without indicating the working schedule. The employee would stay on call in case the employer might need the worker. Workers were paid only for the hours actually worked.

Case law seems to hold this kind of contract void. The Belgian Supreme Court, in a recent decision (16 March, 199, *Rechtskundig Weekblad*, 1992–93, 401) states that a contract stipulating an availability of the worker of between 0 and 40 hours a week is void and would not entitle the worker to full 40 hours of pay if the worker did not actually perform that many hours, even though the worker remained at the disposal of the employer.

B. Home Work. Even though home workers are mentioned in a number of statutory provisions, there is no specific regulation of the contract of employment for home workers. Home work is generally considered to be work performed not on the employer's premises but on a place freely chosen by the employee Most often this is the employee's home.

Most legal scholars shared the opinion that the home worker would be covered by the protective provisions of the Act of 3 July 1978 concerning contracts of employment (including its provisions on termination of contracts), but the Belgian Supreme Court held the opposite based an a dubious interpretation of the Act, referring to legislative history (Supreme Court, 30 November 1992, *Rechtskundig Weekblad*, 1992–93, 851).

Research in the past has shown that those involved in home work tend to be underpaid women who engage in this kind of work to escape unemployment and out of a genuine need for every bit of income possible. (Unpublished report by A. Van Luijcken president of a private working group dealing with home work in the province of Brabant, The Netherlands) The recent Supreme Court case makes an appeal for new legislation and regulation more urgent than ever.

While home work may be an opportunity to combine family responsibilities with work responsibilities, more careful regulations seem to be necessary in order to avoid abuses disturbing family life. A number of high profile home work projects have been introduced recently, involving skilled well paid work, such as translators in insurance companies. Contractual provisions granted the home workers some additional protection. The reason for starting the projects involved more the avoidance of traffic problems than an adaptation to family life and responsibilities.

D. Working Time Arrangements

A. Night Work and Equal Treatment

Night work is work performed between 8 p.m. and 6 a.m. Night work is prohibited in general.

The working hour limits are 10 p.m. and 5 a.m. or 11 p.m. and 6 a.m. for male employees who are 16 years old and female workers who work in continuous operations or in shift work.

Youngsters and women are not allowed to work at night, except in sectors or in functions determined by Royal Decree. For male workers the Labor Act of 16 March 1971 provides a number of explicit exceptions to the prohibition of night work. It is clear that there are a much larger number of exceptions to the general prohibition for male than for female workers and that completely different procedures apply.

With regard to the prohibition of night work for women, recent European developments need to be taken into account. In light of the *Stoeckel* Case – dealing with a French legislative and criminally sanctioned prohibition of night work for women only – handed down by the European Court of Justice (Case No. 345/89 *Criminal Proceedings against Alfred Stoeckel*, 25 July 1991, in ECR, 1991, 4047), and the European Union Commission's demand for the Member States to revoke the ratification of the Convention No 89 concerning Night work of Women Employed in Industry (International Labour Organization), the Belgian government revoked its ratification. This happened on 27 February 1992. At that time the Belgian Government asked the European Commission for a one year period that would allow Belgium to bring national law into compliance.

The present Minister of Labor, Miet Smet, very much concerned with all issues of equality of treatment of the sexes, started the proceedings aimed at the ratification of ILO Convention No 171 concerning Night Work, 1990. (See: *Int'l Ency. Lab. L. & Indus. Rel.*, Kluwer, Deventer, Vol. Codex, I, ILO- 450) The Ministerial proposal would introduce a general prohibition of night work, with limited exceptions. These exceptions would be determined both in the (proposed) legislative act itself, and by Royal Decree. The Minister considered, as a basic premise, that night work is unhealthy and detrimental to family and social life. Out of this concern, night work would be allowed only if necessary for social, humanitarian reasons and for urgent economic reasons.

The social partners, however, did not particularly like the text as proposed by the Minister. One of the reasons probably being the fact that the general prohibition on night work, may impose difficulties with regard to the presently admitted forms of shift work for men. Trade unions and employer organizations came up with a proposal in the National Labor Council. They suggest a text that is closer to the text of the present law. The conformity of the proposed text with the European Community requirements of equality of treatment is debatable.

The current Belgian legal provisions dealing with night work have in the meantime been held to be in contradiction with European law requirements:

> 'Article 5 of the Council Directive 76/207/EEC of 9 February 1976 on the implementation of the principle of equal treatment for men and women as regards access to employment, vocational training and promotion, and working conditions precluded a Member State which prohibited night-work for both men and women from maintaining divergent systems of derogations which differed principally in respect of the procedure for the adoption of derogations and of the duration of the night-work authorized, if such a difference was not justified by the need to ensure the protection of women, particularly with regard to pregnancy and maternity. Article 5 of the directive could not apply to the extent to which those national provisions were adopted in order to ensure the performance by the Member State of obligations arising under an international agreement concluded with non-member countries before the entry into force of the EEC Treaty.' (Case C-13/93, *Office National de l'Emploi v. M. Minne*, 3 February 1994, not yet published in *ECR*).

B. Working Time – Flexibility – Annualization of Working Time – Shift Work
Employer demands were at the origin of this form of working time flexibilization. Concerns over the ability to harmonize working and family were not in the picture.

Annual Working Time – Annualization. The Social Recovery Act of 22 January 1985 introduced the concept of annualization of working time. The normal daily and weekly limits of work (8 hours and 40 hours respectively) can be exceeded on the condition that a legally binding collective bargaining agreement exists that contains provisions on the following:

- the average weekly working time, as well as the total number of hours over a period of 12 consecutive months;
- the number of hours during which work can be performed, below or above the daily limit, without exceeding, however, 2 hours a day and without exceeding a daily working time of 9 hours:
- the number of hours during which the work can be performed, below or above the weekly limit, without exceeding, however, 5 hours a day or 45 hours a week.

Specific rules apply to determine what hours could be considered working hours, with regard to public holidays, hours lost to mechanical breakdowns etc.

Overtime regulations may differ according to the applicable working time schedule. The social partners have recurrently expressed a willingness to reduce overtime in an effort to redistribute available labor. (See *supra*)

New and Flexible Working Patterns. An agreement reached in the National Labor Relations Council on 23 March 1986 called for Parliament to vote an Act on institutionalizing prior working time experiments (Hansenne-experiments, named after the then Minister of Employment). The Parliamentary Act of 17 March 1987 and the national inter-industry wide collective bargaining agreement N. 42 of 2 June 1987, allow 12 hour working days, also for economic reasons, Sunday work, and night work for economic reasons for men. The Parliamentary Act determines that the working time schemes so introduced should have a positive impact on employment.

Shift Work with Night Work. This agreement is applicable to employers employing workers performing in systems of continuous, semi-continuous and fixed night work (enterprises working 24 hours a day) between 11 p.m. and 6 a.m. In principle only employees with an individual contract of employment for an indefinite period of time may perform under these kinds of working time systems. Participation is voluntary. The above mentioned working time systems have to be the result of a collective bargaining agreement with the trade union delegations represented in the enterprise.

Pregnant women may request not to participate in any of the above mentioned systems of working time and this

a) for a period starting three months before the estimated date of birth until at least three months after giving birth; or
b) when, there is a necessity, based on a medical certificate
   - during other periods of the pregnancy or
   - in a period of time to be determined by the doctor and situated in time, more than three months after giving birth.

The request should be in writing.

The Collective Bargaining Agreement No. 46 also deals with transportation, remuneration, weekly working time, compensatory rest, rights of trade union delegations, training, hygiene, occupational safety and medicine, and social infrastructure.

A lot of provisions allow collectively bargained alterations at the level of the sector and/or the enterprise.

E. Recent Government Measures Encouraging all Sorts of Work Distribution

A. National Government Measures. Recent government measures aimed at strengthening Belgium's competitive position include provisions dealing with working time. After an unsuccessful period of time during which the social partners tried to reach an overall agreement on reducing the cost of labor in an effort to combat rising unemployment and an expanding economic recession, government itself stepped in.

Government provided a framework for the redistribution of available labor. Eight ways of redistributing available labor are mentioned. Joint Committees can enter into collective bargaining agreements, determining what measures they think to be most appropriate.

'Company plans' for the redistribution of available labor can be established by collective (bargaining) agreement.

The general framework for redistribution of available labor states that at least one of the following measures should be implemented

- voluntary part-time work with split of available jobs;
- reduction of working time;
- reduction of overtime;
- introduction of a right to educational leave and/or reduction of performances;
- introduction of a system of part-time pre-pension;
- introduction of shift work;
- introduction of flexible working time patterns;
- introduction of the 4-day working week.

All these measures need to be accompanied by additional hiring.

Additional measures can be introduced at the level of the joint committee and at the level of the individual company. If approved by the government a company plan that results in a net increase of employment, may lead to certain benefits for the employer, namely a reduction in social security costs.

The results of bargaining at the level of the industry or branch are presently still meager. Around the end of the month of May the Minister of Employment reported that around 812,278 workers would be included in some form of company plan.

B. Regional Flemish Government. The Flemish government has started a campaign to induce workers, within the framework of the above mentioned company plans, to accept part-time employment. Under the general heading of two slogans, an entire campaign is being set up. The campaign is being subject to a lot of criticism since it seems to portray women in their typical stereotypical behavior as taking care of the children, while men are portrayed as professionals who want to reach higher professional levels through continuing vocational training.

The two main slogans used in the campaign 'And what if you were paid to take it a little easier?' and 'Part-time Work? Full-time life' seem to suggest that the basic aim was to promote quality of life among employees. However, the fact that the campaign fits within the larger framework of company plans aimed at re-distributing the available labor suggests the opposite. Those who accept part-time employment will receive a monthly premium of 5,000-BF (± US$ 147) gross per month if the employee start working half-time work and 3,000-BF (± US$ 88) per month if working hours are reduced to between 51% and 80% of full time employment.

2. Career Breaks and Leaves

A. Justified Leave of Absence

The 1978 Act concerning individual contracts of employment holds that employees are entitled to leave of absence with pay on the occasion of important family events and for the performance of certain civic duties. A Royal Decree determines the events and the number of days justified absence to be granted for each event. For example: in the case of marriage, the employee is entitled to 2 days off (with pay), chosen by the worker during the week of the marriage or during the week following; in the case of election to a jury the employee is entitled to the time necessary, with a maximum of 5 days.

Other events mentioned in the Royal Decree are: marriage of a child of the employee, marriage of a brother, sister, brother-in-law, stepmother, ordination or entry into a monastery or convent of a child, a brother, sister, brother or sister-in-law of the employee; confinement of the wife of the employee; death of the wife and of close relatives (including grandparents); first holy communion of a child; participation of a child in the celebration of the day of 'free-thinking (= non-religious) youth' ; time spent in the army recruitment and selection center; presence of a conscientious objector in the administrative health service; presence at a meeting of the family council convened by a Justice of the Peace; participation in (political) election procedures; adoption of a child. Part-time employees have proportional rights.

B. Leave for Compelling Reasons

Collective Bargaining Agreement No 45, rendered generally binding by Royal Decree (6 March 1990) and article 30*bis* of the Act of 3 July 1978 on contracts of employment grant all employees the right to leave of absence without pay, for compelling reasons.

A compelling reason is an unforeseen event, having no connection with the job as such, demanding the intervention of the employee, in as much as the execution of the contract of employment would prevent the employee's intervention. One can, for example, think of the hospitalization of the employee's spouse, or person living together with the employee, his or her children, parents or grandparents, major damage to the employee's house, such as caused by a fire and so on. The employer and the employee can mutually agree on other reasons they will consider to be compelling reasons justifying the employee's absence.

The employee has the right to be absent for the period allowing the worker to overcome these problems. The periods of absence due to compelling reasons may not extend beyond 10 working days per calendar year.

C. Interruption of the Professional Career

This form of suspension of the performance of the contract of employment was first introduced by the 1985 Social Recovery Act, also with the aim of redistributing available work. A national Collective Bargaining Agreement (No 56) grants the employees a limited right to an interruption of the Professional Career, and this from 1 January 1994 on. The rule under the 1985 Parliamentary Act does not give employees an absolute right and requires the consent of the employer.

Statistics show that from 1991 on, 1% of the active population made use of the possibilities of interrupting the professional career. The success of this formula led to the conclusion of inter-industry wide Collective Bargaining Agreement No 56 that establishes a limited right to interruption of the professional career. Prior to this national collective bargaining agreement coming into existence, several industry wide collective bargaining agreements had already established a similar right to the interruption of the professional career. These industry-wide agreements, however, often restricted the grant of the interruption to certain events and circumstances such as the birth of a child, the adoption of a child or the preparation of pension rights, just to name a few.

Presently the employee is entitled to stop working for a given period of time while receiving a certain financial compensation, to be determined and paid by the Government. The government only contributes financially though if the employee concerned is replaced by an unemployed worker. Reduction of working time to the level of half-time work is equally possible as a form of interruption of the professional career.

The employee who wishes to interrupt his/her career must make a request in writing to the employer 3 months in advance. The suspension must be at least 3 months and not more than 1 year. The total of the duration of the interruption of the professional career on the basis of the national collective bargaining agreement may not exceed three years, over the complete professional career of the employee. Upon using up his/her rights based on the national collective bargaining agreement the employee can still rely on the provisions of the 1985 Parliamentary Act.

The number of employees that can take an interruption in their professional career is restricted to 1% of the average number of employees employed by the employer during the previous calendar year.

An employer that refuses such an interruption within the limits of the rights granted is subject to criminal sanctions. An employer who grants a request for interruption of the professional career, but does not replace the worker on interruption, can be fined by the government unemployment services. The fine will be a lump sum payment for each unreplaced employee per month of nonobservance of the replacement rule.

Sectorial rules contained in sector wide collective bargaining agreements of a specific period of time, could remain in force, even when the rights these collective bargaining agreements provided were less beneficial to the employees than what is presently foreseen in the national collective bargaining agreement. A number of bargaining agreements had a more restricted field of application since they granted workers an entitlement to interruption of their professional career only in cases of child birth or adoption and thus not in general. A large number of such collective bargaining agreements exists. (See: Lehmann, E. & Kohnenmergen, S. 'Analyse de la C.C.T. n. 56 du 13 juillet 1993 instituant un droit limité à l'intéruption de carrière professionelle'(analysis of Collective Bargaining Agreement No 56 of 13 July 1993 instituting a limited right to interruption of the professional career), *Orientations*, 1994, 59 *et seq.*)

D. Paid Educational Leave

The 1985 Social Recovery Act replaced the 1973 Act on Credit Hours and reorganized the system by which an employee can be absent from work in order to follow certain courses while retaining salary. The Act foresees in a maximum number of hours a year, during which an employee can be absent for vocational training (240 hours) or for general education (160 hours) (240 hours if the employee follows within the same year both a general and a vocational course).

The employee who wishes to exercise a right to paid educational leave has to inform the employer in writing specifying the courses he/she will follow and indicating the envisaged absences.

The organization of paid educational leave in each enterprise is in the hands of the works council. When there is no works council the matter is dealt with by union delegation. In the absence of the latter the employer directly deals with the employees. In organizing the leave, the council has to take both the needs of work organization in the enterprise as well as the interests and specific situations of each employee into account.

A recent statutory amendment (Act of 10 June 1993) establishes the prevalence of the collective planning over the individual one. In the event of a controversy over the planning, the case is submitted to the Social Inspection of the Ministry of Employment and Labor, which will first try to mediate and if necessary take a decision.

The number of employees, performing the same jobs in the enterprise, making use of their right to educational leave is restricted by law. The employer may oppose more than 10% of the employees making use of their right at the same time, under the restrictions mentioned above.

The Ministry of Employment and Labor refunds the employer for the wages and social security contributions, which the employer is obliged to pay to the employee, who is on paid educational leave:

- 50% in the case of occupational training;
- 100% in the case of general education. The remuneration level is capped. Indexation will start from 1 September 1995.

These payments are financed by a special social security contribution paid by all employers.

IV. REMOVING EXISTING INEQUALITIES

1. Positive Actions

Positive actions are defined as actions aimed at removing real inequalities disadvantageously affecting women's opportunities in employment. Such actions will be carried out by means of equal opportunity plans comprising measures to reduce the prejudicial consequences for women arising out of traditional social situations and attitudes or measures to promote women's presence and participation in working life in all sectors and occupations and at all levels of the hierarchy. (See: Royal decree containing measures for the promotion of equal opportunities for men and women in the private sector, 14 July 1987 (amended in 1993), *Int'l Ency. Lab. L. & Indus. Rel.*, Kluwer, Deventer, Vol. Legislation, Legislation Belgium, Act. n. 40, 541.)

Equal opportunity plans can be drawn up at the level of the industry or at enterprise level. One example of an industry engaging in an approach of positive action is the chemical industry.

While there is massive unemployment, there is at the same time an increased need for skilled labor. Human Resources management in the chemical industry is paying increased attention to female labor as a solution to the skill shortages that sector of industry is experiencing. The chemical industry is suffering from a sustained shortage of skilled labor and is therefore prepared to take positive measures to increase the percentage of skilled women. (See: Janssens de Bisthoven, A. and Bernage, M. and De Ceuster, P., 'Vrouwen tussen bescherming en carriere' (women between protection and career), in *Tendenzen in het Bedrijfsrecht*, Kluwer Antwerp, 1991, 211 *et seq.*) A network of positive action plans for women has been set up within the chemical industry. The Ministry of Labor is in charge of the coordination of the plans. Other sectors of industry engage in similar activities.

Whether positive actions lead to any permanent results may be largely dependent on the specific situations of a given industry or company. A thorough evaluation of the positive action plans that were installed is presently underway.

2. Council for Equal Opportunities

Within the Ministry of Employment a Council for Equal Opportunities has been established. (See: Royal Decree, 15 February 1993 concerning the establishment of a council for equal opportunities, *Off. Gaz.*, 6 March 1993.) The purpose of this Council is to actively contribute in the effort to eradicate all forms of direct and indirect discrimination against women and to create an equality in fact between men and women. To that extent the Council can engage in studies, draft proposals and report on it for the National Labor Council, etc.

3. Positive Action and the Social Partners

Given the importance of the social partners in determining working conditions, through collective bargaining and their active participation in the various systems of employee participation, female participation *within* the social partners (trade unions and employer association) is of the utmost importance.

Looking at the participation rate of women in the different employee representative councils at the various levels of industrial relations in Belgium, one cannot but note the underrepresentation of women. (See: Cornelis, C., 'De vrouwen in de sociale verkiezingen' (Women in the social elections), in *Arbeidsblad*, 1993, June issue, 26 *et seq.*)

A new legislative proposal incites the trade unions to insure proportional representation of female employees on the voting lists to be introduced in the companies for the social elections, according to the female participation rate in the company's work force.

4. Positive Action in the Field of Continuing Vocational Training

Another effort aimed at stimulating more qualitative participation of women in the labor market is set up by the social partners jointly. Since 1988, the social partners, in their inter-industry wide collective bargaining agreements dedicated a certain percentage of the wage bill to continued vocational training. At the beginning 0.18% of the total wage bill, for the 1993 and 1994 period, up to 0.25% and 0.30% respectively (See: Blanpain, R., Maroy, C. and Engels, C., 'Belgium', in Contractual Policies concerning continued vocational training in the European Community Member States, Blanpain, R., Engels, C. and Pellegrini, C. (eds.), Peeters, Leuven, 1994, 103 *et seq.*, 108.) The money so obtained is used to organize training for what is referred to as the 'risk groups', containing people who have low skills, who have been unemployed for a long period of time, who are re-entering the labor market after a long period of absence, etc. Women make more use of the different forms of (extended) leave that are offered and are proportionally overrepresented in the group of low skilled employees and those re-entering the labor market after an extended period of absence. The continuing vocational training provided for in the inter-industry wide collective bargaining agreement will enhance qualitative participation. Some of the funds have also been used to set up pilot programs for positive action and child care.

V. MEASURES SURROUNDING EMPLOYMENT – CHILD CARE PROVISIONS – CARE FOR THE ELDERLY

1. Government Support

Provisions for child care are, on the face of it, sex blind. Granting child care benefits is not dependent on the female or male identity of the parent. However, taking into account that the burdens of family life weigh unequally heavy on women, any alleviation of these burdens is likely to have a much larger impact on the female labor force and the ability of women workers to harmonize their working and family life than on their male counterparts.

Government, both national and regional, has understood the importance of child care for an equal and harmonious participation of men and women in the work force. Also both sides of industry seem to have come to grips with the problem of child care. In the inter-industry wide agreement of 1993–1994 the social partners agreed to dedicate 0.05% of the total wage bill to child care. It seems that the same effort will also be extended over the 1995–1996 period.

The projects that obtain government funding will have to live up to certain conditions. While most of the effort seems, at least at present, still dedicated to organizing child care for smaller children (below the age of 3), more attention also seems to be going in the direction of establishing services to look after older children for the periods of time they are not in school.

A look at some data concerning the Flemish part of the country may give an idea about how much is actually being organized at present, and this primarily under the impetus of an institution called 'Kind en Gezin' (child and family). Research showed that in the year 1993, 53.7% of all children between the age of 3 months and 3 years, used some form of child care at least once a week. It is striking that for the larger part of them the grandparents and close relatives are taking on child care activities (about 45%). About 42.5% of all children receive care in centers and families supported and/or subsidized by the institution 'Kind en Gezin'.

The organization of these forms of child care is such that apart from the government contribution or subsidy, the parents of the child contribute according to their income. Low income families are thus not excluded from what – if offered privately – often is a very expensive service. Low income families pay around US$ 2 a day, while parents in the highest income bracket may pay up to US$ 18 a day for the care of their child.

It should be mentioned furthermore, that the payments parents make for the child care services, are to a certain extent tax deductible expenses. This means that the actual cost involved in child care is even less than the parents' personal contribution to the child care center.

The organization Child and Family subsidized up to 30,400 opportunities for child care. An additional 10,500 instances of child care are approved in close contact with the organization, even though they are not subsidized as such. These numbers are very impressive, taking into account that during the year 1993 only 68,379 babies were born in the Flemish part of the country.

2. Private Employer Insurance

An important supporting private initiative in this regard deals with the ability of employers to insure themselves against the cost of employees being absent from work due to their children's illness. The insurance will provide the employee with a baby-sitter in case the child is sick and has to stay home e.g. from school. Such a form of insurance would be a very useful addition to the various already existing schemes of child support, since sick children are almost never welcome in the child care centers. Employees have a limited right to leave for compelling reasons (see *supra*). However, this form of leave, is a leave without pay and is restricted in time. There is also an employer's cost involved in the absence of the permanent worker, since his/her absence makes the use of temporary labor inevitable for their employer.

The new insurance offered by the company 'Europe Assistance' seems to be a convenient solution to this problem. If the child gets sick during the night, the employee calls up the employer in the morning. The latter will then contact the insurance company. The same day or the following day a baby-sitter will be at the disposal of the worker.

The premium the employer will have to pay for the insurance will be calculated in accordance to the total number of children the employer's work force has. The contract with the insurance company is supposed to cover the whole work force, and not just a particular segment of it. (See: 'verzekering voor oppas ziek kind' (insurance for baby-sitting sick child), *Het Nieuwsblad*, 20 May 1994.)

3. Care for the Elderly

Equally important as child care will become institutions and measures dealing with care for the elderly. Some existing legal provisions on leave already grant some opportunities in this regard. (see *supra*)

However, in the whole debate on the harmonization of working life and family life as it has been going on in Belgium, the issue of care for the elderly has not been granted a very central place. Without a doubt, more attention will have to be paid to these problems in the near future.

VI. CONCLUDING REMARKS

Government has a role of overriding importance to play in creating a working environment that allows and stimulates equal employment opportunities for both sexes and that will as a consequence allow an improved co-existence between family life and working life.

In the first instance, government has to introduce rules that guarantee equal treatment in employment, such as equal pay, equal opportunities for promotion etc. While these ground rules are in place in Belgium, actual enforcement of them may still be a problem. The reversal of the burden of proof in sex discrimination cases would facilitate enforcement of the legislative provisions. However, the issue of reversing the burden of proof is subject to political debate and is far from resolved.

The bare equal treatment rules need to be supplemented, however, by rules that are aimed at creating equality in fact. Certain amendments to general and prima facie sex-blind measures will have to be made in order to ensure the fairness of their application to people in fact not so equally situated. And indeed, women and men still are not equally situated when dealing with the 'burdens' of family life. Women, even when actively participating in the work force still unequally share in the burdens of family life.

With this as a background observation, the whole evolution in the direction of creating increased flexibility through the encouragement of e.g. part-time work and flexibility in working time arrangements may not have the positive effect one would be hoping for. The flexibility that is granted through part-time jobs, flexible contracts like home work and on-call contracts, through the various working time schemes, etc. concerns, to a very large extent the lower skilled, lower paid jobs. Women workers predominantly perform jobs of this kind. Since their activity 'would allow', due to its flexible nature, a combination of different functions and activities of family life, the burdens of the latter more often fall on the women. And as a result women will get stuck in the more flexible, but also low skilled low paid jobs.

Increased flexibility may also have a positive impact on the ability of harmonizing working and family life. However, it will not necessarily have this effect. This should not come as a surprise, since most of the measures that were studied above, were not specifically introduced in Belgium with the purpose of alleviating the difficulties of combining working and family life. Most measures under discussion were not introduced out of a concern for the individual employee's ability to cope with both working and family life, but to grant employers and enterprises an increased degree of flexibility in their personnel management. Other measures are aimed at increasing the number of those with a job. The effect of these measures on family life was seen as a secondary impact at best.

A number of other measures go more directly to the heart of the matter: positive actions to upgrade female employment, increased female participation in employee representation, granting different forms of leave etc.

What may be of equal, if not of higher importance, may be 'institutions' surrounding working life such as child care institutions.

However, the most important factor in the whole debate, will be a fundamental change of ideas about how both sexes should participate in working life and in family life. Something not to be achieved by the mere passing of any legislative act.

France

Jean-Claude Javillier

INTRODUCTORY REMARKS

Scope

It would be quite impossible, in a few pages, to give a general and comprehensive overview of the very complex and important issue of the harmonisation of family and working within the French legal system. The author wants only to stress some general elements in order to underline general trends especially related to labour law. The report will include two parts. Briefly stated, the first part describes general elements about the social and economic background of this very important problem which will be analysed. The second part includes technical elements regarding the evolution of the legal policies.

METHOD

To fully analyse the ways of harmonising work and family life, one would have to cover very different methodologies and academic areas, which for a French professor of law is quite impossible. One has to consider not only law, but also economics, history, sociology, psychology, etc. From the legal point of view only, it has to be stressed that we have to take into account not only private law (which includes labour law and social security law) but also public law (which includes for example, administrative law, budgetary matters, state and local involvement in support service). In the first part of this article, the analysis will focus on general tendencies; that is to say stressing the complementary nature of all the methods mentioned above. In the second part, the analysis is mainly on labour law.

PERSPECTIVES

As the end of the 20th century comes closer, great social changes are occurring. The world is changing so quickly and profoundly, that it is impossible to know how far this analysis does not pertain to old 'world' ideas. At times it seems we are reproducing our habits of thinking onto many contemporary issues, rather than giving a true and comprehensive view of the questions we are trying to analyse. A prime example is the concept of family, which in French society has been in big trouble for decades, as in other European countries. The cultural and economic contexts have changed so much that the terminology previously used no longer carries with it the same meaning across different generations. Such radical changes affect the value of work itself and younger generations are considering the function of work and their participation at the workplace in a new light.

One has to avoid any temptation to give a biased view of the issues, and especially to avoid being under the influence of some 'mood' or 'fad'. The media, including television images and radio messages, has a growing impact on society. In this 'media society' weeks or even years are a very long period in the minds and memories of journalists and politicians. Consequently, our society tends to emphasize some elements which quickly lose importance over time. There is a risk in thinking that societies and law are quickly changing. On the contrary, human beings in the contemporary world may be more reluctant than it seems to change their habits or to adapt themselves to the new way of life. There is quite a mystery in the way we modify our analyses, our customs and practices. However, resisting change should not necessarily be considered a conservative approach to life. Perhaps it's just that we are continually and slowly establishing a new equilibrium in social life.

Women, as well as men, employers, as well as trade unions and workers' representatives – are hesitant in their analysis and strategies of the important issues of harmonising work and family life. There is no one solution, no simple technique (especially regarding the law) which can be used in order to find a general solution to the very complicated questions which are reported and analysed further on.

PART I: GENERAL POLICY AND EVOLUTION OF SOCIETY

Both work and family life have changed dramatically during the 20th century, leaving great uncertainty on these issues, as well as on many others at the end of this century.[1] It seems useful to give a broad overview of the effects which arise from these changes.

A. Work and Family Life in the Cultural Context

A major change in the labour market has been the increased participation of women in all areas of production and services.[2] Many explanations for this can be given for countries such as France. The transformation of the education system and the stride towards equality between men and women are among the factors which can explain this evolution. From a legal point of view, one must stress the impact of European law, from the beginning of the European community until the present European Union.

All these changes have been supported by unions as well as by feminist activists, even though in France the feminist movement is not as strong and developed as in many countries, especially compared with North American countries during the latter part of this century.

Another element which has to be carefully analysed is the relation between men and women and especially their attitude towards their respective roles in soci-

---

1. See Secrétariat d'Etat au Plan, *Entrer dans le XXI ème siècle. Essai sur l'avenir de l'identité française*, Introduction de Emmanuel Le Roy Ladurie, Avant-Propos de Lionel Stoleru: *La Découverte / La Documentation Française*, Paris, 1990, spéc, *Trois institutions directement mises á l'éprouve, La famille incertaine*, pp. 121–122.
2. Women comprise approximately more than 40% of the workforce in the majority of the OECD countries (see 'Towards a service sector economy and an increasingly female labour force' *in Women and structural change. New Perspectives*: OECD, Paris, 1994, at p. 48. For a world-wide view see ILO Le travail dans le monde, Geneva, 1992, at 22 *et. seq.*

ety. A widely held assumption has been that a great difference exists between Northern European countries and Southern European countries. The traditional view was that in Southern European countries the men were the sole wage earners working outside the home and women 'worked' at home, their primary tasks being related to child rearing. This traditional view is changing, and people in Southern European countries are changing their views on the old, strong separation between the sexes regarding their activities in society. On the streets of Paris and other major French cities, one can now see fathers carrying their babies as they go shopping, although maybe still not as often as in Nordic countries A swing back toward more traditional values can also be detected among younger generations. The traditional concept of family is coming back, possibly with some traditional separation between the father and the mother regarding jobs and activities. But, at the same time there great instability within the family structure, most notably in the amount of divorces. Divorce is happening so often that one may consider that parents married for a long time who have children represents a very atypical situation.

B. Family Life and Work in an Economic Context

It is very important to take into account the existing relations between social values, cultural habits and economic situations. From an economic point of view, things are changing very much in Europe. Generally speaking, the situation of women is not the same as it was even as recent as ten years ago. The organization of society is simultaneously moving towards a two-wage-earning family and also towards a single-wage-earning family. Many married couples have both partners who work outside the home, and single parents are also working outside home, which often creates big problems when there are children to care for. These working and parenting arrangements have created opportunities for institutions at plant level, such as works councils, and have gained in importance to workers. A traditional social action (*activité sociale*)[3] of the works councils (*comité d'entreprise*) is to be in charge of holiday centres or caring for babies and very young children.[4] It may also be that the works council gives funds to local authorities in order to increase the number of beds in special institutions for child care; thus creating an option for workers to leave their babies in such an institution. The works council can also give enterprise workers special benefits (*primes*) in order to compensate for the price of child care, which is quite expensive.[5]

The current economic climate very often induces continuous stress upon people and has a strong influence on social attitudes. Anybody having any qualifications and rank in an enterprise, fears rising unemployment. Obviously, the fact that both parents are working is due to the fact that one wage is not enough, especially to live in big cities, to rent flats in cities such as Paris or Lyon or to pay for private or even public child care services.

---

3. There is no limitation by the labour code (section R. 432–2), the *comité d'entreprise* can create and organize all kinds of social benefits in favor of the workers and their families. There are some examples of these activities given in the Labour Code.
4. According to statistics given in 1992 some 241 crèches were managed by works councils a well as employers, in France where had been admitted 15,250 children (S. Cohen, citée par M. Cohen in *Le droit des comités d'entreprise et des comités de groupe*, LGDJ, Paris 3e édition, 1994, at 598 note 93.
5. There are always some difficulties regarding the situation of the benefits given by the works council regarding the social security system. The benefit give by the works councils is not within certain very limited conditions, submitted to the social security payments (see Lettre ministérielle du 2 juillet 1992 et circulaire A.C.O.S.S. du 29 Juillet 1992).

PART 2: LABOUR POLICY AND LAW REFORMS

The characteristics of a particular industrial relations system, as well as the entire legal system has to be fully taken into account when one tries to stress some technical questions related to the workplace and more generally employment in a country. The state interventions remain among the most important characteristics of the French system, in spite of some changes during the 80's. The labour code is the legal pillar regarding labour relations. That is not to say that collective bargaining has no impact; its importance has been growing during the past decade. But collective agreements are subject to many regulations which cannot be avoided (*ordre public*) and also in practical terms, collective bargaining is of a secondary importance in industrial relations. State regulations or unilateral (employer's) rules are at the core of industrial relations as well of work practices at plant level.

During the past years, under both socialist and liberal governments, flexibility has been a major topic of discussion. In the 80's, the issue was discussed in a manner traditional in French political affairs: whatever was said by left or the right necessarily had to be opposed by whatever party was on the opposite of the political spectrum. After a period of domination by the left, during which they captured the whole political power to decide through the President of the Republic and the Prime Minister, the government now shares the power since the Prime Minister is a liberal (R.P.R.). Everyone wants to improve employment; in order to do so, almost everyone thinks that some flexibility has to be developed or at least to be maintained in the Labour Code. The issue of flexibility is linked to the issues being analysed in this article. For example, flexibility is realized through part-time jobsharing, flexible working hours, etc. These rules not only affect the whole employment market, but also can have a positive impact on the harmonisation between working life and family life. Some analysts stress that upon closer examination of the practical situation, an atmosphere of discrimination exists: namely that women, much more than men, are using these new rules which promote flexibility of employment, and women are more frequently in precarious situations. Discrimination could be growing under the guise, although the French Labour Code, as well as the European Law is strongly fighting against it. But, is there any regulation without any negative effects, no matter how significant or insignificant? It is a harsh reality that what may be better from an economic or legal point of view, can make practical situations worse from a human or social point of view.

Taking a place among the technical instruments used to fight unemployment, it should be stressed that the new orientation of the past and present Government has been to create new employment in the service sector. But this matter should be studied from another technical point of view: the tax system. Every year, the tax bill includes special measures which allow the parents, and more generally those who have dependent children, to benefit from a tax reduction. One example is the possibility to deduct the expenses for child care outside the home up to a maximum of 25% of the amount of money spent within a certain limit.[6] In some instances the maximum tax deduction given is up to to 50%.[7]

---

6. Generally speaking, this is between 10,000 and 30,000 FF.
7. With a maximum amount as mentioned above.

A. Maternity and Paternity Leaves

For quite some time, pregnancy and maternity have been a cause of suspension of the contract of employment under the Labour Code (section L. 122–25). A minimum period of suspension given by the Code; the duration of the leave depends on different elements. The same rules are not implemented in case of adoption of a child. The rules do not contradict the new Directive from the European Union passed in 1992.[8] Some modifications include, for example, the right to realize a *bilan de compétence* (balance of personal knowledge and job situation)[9] (new section 122–28–7) to adapt oneself to the working technologies and practices before coming back to work (section L. 122–28).[10]

A very important question and also quite complex from a legal point of view, is to determine the situation towards end of the suspension of the contract of employment. If the woman wants to work again the labour code says that the employer has to give her the same job or an equivalent one (section L. 122–26).

The general policy has been to extend the right to suspend the contract employment in order to facilitate child care and education. Since an Act of 4 January 1984, under certain conditions[11] the worker can ask for a new suspension or a switch to work part-time. It is also possible to shift freely from part-time work and parental leave. The mother, as well as the father (even if the mother does not so request) can ask for a parental leave or for a reduction of working hours.[12] Both father and mother can ask for such a working time reduction. The Labour Code sets out in detail the (very formal) procedure to be implemented when the employee makes such requests. The employer has three weeks to give an answer; afterwards the agreement is considered to be given (section L. 122–28–4). At the end of the parental leave, the employer has to give the employee the same job, or a similar job with a similar wage. Regarding the seniority rights, according to the provisions of the Labour Code, half of the duration of the parental leave will be considered as working periods (section L. 122–28–6).

The legal, social and psychological situation is not the same across large enterprises, or medium or small sized enterprises.[13] When there are less than 100 workers employed in the enterprise, the employer has the right to oppose the parental leave requested under certain conditions. First the employer has to consult the

8. The Introduction of Measures to Encourage Improvements in the Safety and Health at Work of Pregnant Workers who have recently given Birth or are Breastfeeding (Tenth Individual Directive within the Meaning ofArticle 16(1) of Directive 89/391/EEC), 92/85/EEC, 19 October 1992.

9. This a 'new right' in order to facilitate mobility and qualification of the workers which has been introduced by the Social Partners in the collective agreements and by the Parliament in the law regarding economic dismissal during recent years.

10. These training facilities are taken into account for the compulsory financial participation of the employer to the professional training at plant level (new section L. 951–1, para. 6).

11. Such as at least one year seniority with the same employer, the child is under three years old or if adopted, the child has been with the family for less than three years.

12. The working time per week has to be at least 32 hours when the legal working time in force is 39 hours.

13. See. G. Von Potobsky, *Small and medium-sized enterprises and labour law, 131 International Labour Review* 603 (1992). *Bulletin of Comparative Labour Relations*, no. 26 (1993), R. Blanpain and M. Biagi, eds. J.-M. Servais, Labour Law in Small and Medium-Sized Enterprises: An Ongoing Challenge, *The International Journal of Comparative Labour Law* 10/2, Summer 1994, at 119.

workers' representatives at plant level, and secondly he has to give a reason for refusing to grant the parental leave (i.e. damaging production and good enterprise management).

There are other provisions of the Labour Code, not related to maternity or adoption, which can permit the man or woman to harmonise family life and working life. For example, there is a sabbatical leave for any kind of personal as well as professional activities (section L. 122–32–17 *et seq.*). But this right is subject to conditions, for example seniority within the enterprise of 36 months, and 6 years of professional activities, and the leave is granted for a duration of between 6 to 11 months.

B. Working Time Arrangements and Part-Time Work

The introduction of flexibility regarding working time is one of the main developments in French Labour Law. It has to be stressed that these changes were supported very clearly and strongly by the employers. The unions have been very reluctant, fearing that the employer could use part-time as a 'Trojan Horse' in the Labour Code by trying to destabilize social protection and to increase precarious conditions of all the workers. Most French unions fought any management attempts to promote the individualization of working conditions as being opposed to collective approach of labour relations, and possibly also as being a class struggle.[14]

In practice, as well as from a legal point of view, the rules concerning part-time and flexible working conditions are of great importance. In order to fight unemployment, governments, as well as the social partners, have established new rules which make these rules easier to use. One has to consider that the new regulations on labour relations are by nature ambiguous. On one hand, the social partners,[15] as well as the legislator, are stressing the need to promote the individual interests of the workers; but on the other hand, they are also using flexibility in labour relations in order to adjust to the enterprise and to avoid collective redundancies. For those who think that Labour Law is always ambiguous, promoting the interest of the employees but also organising the enterprise; such a situation can be considered as 'classical', or provocative, depending of the ideological point of view.[16]

The scope of part-time work has been extended by the Labour Code, since 1982,[17]

14. From many employees' point of view, the negative approach of part-time work, has been the origin of a distance between the unions' analyses and strategies and the daily life of the workers at plant level, and more generally in the whole society. The relationship between the collective approach and the individual perspective on labour relations seems to have changed, in relation to the cultural context. A pragmatic approach is increasingly used by the workers, opposing any ideological and global approach of their situation. This also has to be linked with the increasingly individualistic approach of social life as juxtaposed against a collective and union approach.
15. In an agreement such as the '*accord national interprofessionnel*', 21 March 1989, stressed the need to promote the workers aspirations in order to improve their living conditions.
16. Possibly the situation is different for those who think (or thought) that one can give always a unilateral view of any Labour Law rule. The privilege given to any collective approach, which simplifies and unifies, versus an approach which take in account the particularities of the individual situation in any group, explains why the 'interest' of the worker seems so easy to analyse. The worker is always in a very radical and Manichaeanism opposition with the one of the enterprise, or of the employer (for those who reject the existence of the enterprise as a community itself).
17. Ordonnance n° 82–41 du 16 janvier 1982 (J.O., 17 janvier) passed under a socialist government, with a strong will to promote collective bargaining at national level).

and especially after a new act passed in 1993.[18] Prior to the 1993 reform, working time was considered within a given time frame of the week or the month with more than 1/5 under the legal or collective agreement definition of the duration of work.[19] Since 1993, the part-time working time can also be analysed within the whole year[20] These measures are not limited to the employees under the Labour Code (Private Labour Law relations, contract of employment). For Public Servants, an act passed in July 1994,[21] also has the principle to promote part-time.[22] In order to encourage the employers to recruit new employees, or not to dismiss current ones, the government is frequently using social security incentives, such as reducing the employers contribution under the compulsory social security system.

A new Act, passed in July 1994 is aimed at improving the situation of the family.[23] The government clearly stressed that the political orientation was to promote the interests of the family in the whole of society. The Bill has been modified by Parliament, which has added new rights especially in favour of those who are working part-time in order to care for their children. Generally speaking, there is an extension of the benefits given to parents in order to promote the education of their children. Among the many measures included in the new Act, one can stress the extension of the scope and the amount of some benefits, such as the *allocation parentale d'éducation* (A.P.E.),[24] or the *allocation de garde d'enfant á domicile* (A.G.E.D.).[25]

The new Act introduces new rights for workers. For example, there is a special non-paid leave for 3 days a year[26] which can be used by any worker when a child, less than 16 years old, is ill or has suffered an accident. The Act is also gives the right for workers[27] who are caring for a child in the case of illness, accident or significant handicap, to work part-time for six months, and possibly another period of the same duration.

As happens very often in French Labour Law, reforms are not only the result of the political will and social policy of the Government. In order to generalise some collective agreements and practices at industry or plant level, the Act often takes

18. *Loi n° 93–1313 du 20 décembre 1993, relative á l'emploi*, usually referred to as *loi quinquiennale* (J.O., 21 décembre) (under a liberal government, with a privilege given to collective bargaining at plant level).
19. Within a weekly timeblock of 39 hours of working time, part-time work is less than 32 hours. Within the monthly time block, part-time is less than 136 hours.
20. For an employee working 6 days a week, the annual duration of work has to be under 1451 hours.
21. Loi n° 94–628 du 25 juillet 1994, relative á l'organisation du temps de travail, au recrutement et aux mutations dans la fonction publique (J.O.,, 26 juillet; Cf. synthèse in Liaisons Sociales, Documents, N° 84/94 du 16 août 1994).
22. According to statistics given during the debate at Parliament, at the end of 1992, 162.000 were part-timers (included 34.000 not been full civil servants); half of these civil servants, being employed in the National Education system (from primary school to university).
23. Loi n° 94–629 du 25 juillet 1994, relative á la famille (J.O. 26 juillet; see also synthèse in Liaisons Sociales, Législation sociale, n° 7080 du mercredi 27 juillet 1994).
24. Those who are working, as well as training, part-time, can now also receive these benefits (the amount given by decree for less than 39, 30 hours per week is 1.950 FF) the benefit is given when there is a second child in the family (previously, benefits were granted after the third child); those who are benefiting are included in the old age pension.
25. This benefit is granted to persons employing someone at home to care for a child under 3 years old, and reduced benefits if the child is older. The definition of the professional activity will be broadened by a decree. The amount of the benefit corresponds to the participation fee paid by employees and employers to the social security system. The maximum benefit established by decree is 3,800 FF.
26. If the child is less than one year old, or if there are at least three children under 16 years, the leave is extended to 5 days a year.
27. Subject to certain conditions, such as a seniority in the enterprise of at least one year.

into account the result of experiences, especially those gained through collective bargaining. During the parliamentary debate, a collective agreement signed in May 1994,[28] has been given as a good example of what can be done at plant level to promote the harmonisation between working conditions and family life. It has been decided that every parent with at least one year seniority at the enterprise, will receive a parental leave benefit. The amount of the benefit, given by the enterprise, is the same level as the one given by the family benefits paid by the Social Security system.[29] It is very important to stress that the agreement mentioned above very closely and clearly links the parental leave benefit with promotion of employment at enterprise level. For every worker who has requested a parental leave, the enterprise has the duty to recruit a young unemployed worker (if not full time, then two young people), in order to given them a first time job experience. It also decided that when the worker out on parental leave returns to the job, the employer – depending on the economic situation of the enterprise – will be under unfixed term contract (including the seniority based on the fixed-term contract while replacing the worker under parental leave).

One very interesting and important question had been discussed at Groupe Fleury Michon which is related to the financing or the benefit given in case of parental leave. The employer asked the works council to participate and give money (30%), as well as the enterprise itself (70%). The majority of the works council voted against. But the employer decided to ask directly the workers their opinion on that question[30]; the result was, clearly but not strongly, in favour of the participation of the works council.[31] The employer also asked to the Social Security institution (the 'C.A.F.', mentioned above) to pay the enterprise benefit and also that the enterprise would not have to pay the taxes (employer's as well as employee's fees). Under all these conditions, it has been said that approximately 40 workers (mainly women) would benefit from such a system.

Members of Parliament, wanted the bill on family to include such possibilities as those decided according to the Fleury Michon collective agreement. The benefits given by the employer during the parental leave or the part-time period, are not subject to Social Security fees, under certain conditions, with the same 'spirit' than the agreement above mentioned.[32]

---

28. *Accord du Groupe Fleury Michon du 25 avril 1994, portant sur l'extension expérimentale du congé d'allocation parentale et la création d'une allocation parentale étendue.*
29. For family policy and benefits, there is, in the compulsory and general Security System, a special institution at national and regional levels (Caisses d'Allocations Familiales, C.A.F.). The amount of money given by the C.A.F., for 1994, is established at 2.929 FF.
30. It happens, more frequently nowadays, that the employer wants to use 'direct democracy', in order to be sure that the workers' representatives are not misrepresenting those who are rank and file. Obviously, these management methods are not welcomed by the unions, which are stressing the will of the employers to avoid them, to fight them through direct democracy and individualisation of the working conditions and relations. Generally speaking, workers give their answers from a very pragmatic point of view. Consequently, it appears that on some important issues the workers are in contradiction to with their representatives at plant or enterprise level (union delegates, workers delegates and works council). As usual the workers' representatives stress that the employer is using a terminology and asking questions which are purposely in favour of the workers, avoiding mention of some elements or details which could have negative consequences on the employees' situation.
31. There were 1955 workers as voters; 1694 voted; 791 in favour and 744 against; 159 nor or without opinion voters (see Liaisons Sociales, Législation sociale, n° 7032 du lundi 9 mai 1994, p. 1).
32. The employer has to recruit within a period of 30 days after parental leave or part-time; the number of hours of work for those recruited cannot be less than the one corresponding to the period of parental leave or the part-time; the wage cannot reduced more than the one corresponding to the diminution of the working time.

This article has not covered all the elements directly or indirectly related to the complex problem of harmonising family life and work. It has to be stressed that unlike most legal questions, the intervention of lawyers is not of primary importance in this particular situation. Above all, cultural, economic and social perspectives should directly be taken into account in promoting a policy in favour of harmonisation.

The new dynamic given to such policies, comes from the need to promote new working conditions, greater equality between men and women, and a real understanding of all those who are at the core of the family, parents and children.

REFERENCES

Caisse Nationale d'Allocations Familiales, *Entre la vie professionnelle et la vie familiale: Revue Recherches et Prévisions*, n° 36, Juin 1994, 80 p.
R. Blanpain et J.-C. Javillier, *Droit du Travail communautaire: Librairie Générale de Droit et de Jurisprudence, Collection Droit des Affaires*, Paris, 1991, 282 p.
G. Couturier, *Droit du Travail*: P.U.F., Collection *Droit fondamental*, Tome 1: *Les relations individuelles de travail*, Paris, 2ème éd., 1993, 568 p.
M. Despax and J. Rojot, *France* in *International Encyclopaedia for Labour Law and Industrial Relations*, Ed. R. Blanpain: Kluwer, Deventer, 1987 *et seq*.
G. Guery, *Vivre l'Europe sociale*, Préface de Padraig Flynn: Editions Dunod, Paris, 1994, 275 p.
I.L.O., *World Labour Report – 1994*, esp. Chapter 2: *Promoting harmony between work and family: The role of support services and flexible working arrangements*, pp. 27–42.
I.N.S.E.E., *La société française*, Données sociales, Paris, 1993.
J.-C. Javillier, *Manuel de Droit du Travail*: Librairie Générale de Droit et de Jurisprudence, 4ème éd., 1992, 612 p.
G. Lyon-Caen et J. Pelissier, *Droit du Travail*: Précis Dalloz, 16ème éd., Paris, 1992, 869 p.
O.E.C.D., *Women and Structural Change. New Perspectives*: Paris, 1994, 199 p.
J.E. Ray, *Droit du Travail, Droit vivant*: Editions Liaisons, 3ème éd. Paris, 1993, 393 p.
B. Teyssic, *Droit du Travail*: LITEC, Tome 1/ *Relations individuelles de travail*: 2ème éd., Paris, 1992, 759 p.

Italy

Marco Biagi

1. LEGAL AND CONTRACTUAL REGULATIONS OF WORKING TIME

Regulations of working time, laid down by legislation and/or collective bargaining, also perform a general function of reconciling working life and family life. Although the primary objective is to lay down maximum working hours compatible with the protection of the employee in his/her physical dimension, there is no doubt that arrangements in this area also aim at preserving space for fulfilling family obligations. It is consequently worth looking at the regulations which affect working time in Italy in general.

Needless to say, these general remarks only indirectly relate to the theme of working/family life and their harmonization, but due to the limited development of specific rules in this respect (see below § 4) it seems advisable to cover also this general perspective.

According to art. 36 of Italian Constitution 'the maximum daily hours of work shall be prescribed by law'. The Act N. 692 stating the maximum of 8 hours a day (or, alternatively, 48 hours a week) dates back to 1923 (Ichino 1987). This legal standard has long since become obsolete because the collective agreements have considerable reduced both weekly and daily working time. Rules in this respect are established by national industry-wide agreements. But company-level agreements sometimes reduce working time still further. In the textile industry for example, the sector-level agreement lays down a 40-hour week over five working days while many enterprise-level agreements provide for 36 hours over six.

Union claims across all sectors reflect a concern to reduce working time. As in many other European countries, the idea of reducing working time in order to protect jobs is currently been mooted in Italy against a background of economic crisis (Scarponi 1988). A Governmental project wants to reduce the legal maximum working week from 48 hours to 40. Collectively agreed working time is, of course, already well below the 48-hour level, but statutory overtime payments still start from 48 hours. A reduction in the maximum week to 40 hours would have the effect of making overtime more expensive, thus discouraging its use. Beyond the supposed job-creating (or, at least, job saving) effect, this policy in favour of reducing maximum (statutorily provided or collectively agreed) working hours would allow employees to spend more time with their families. But employers object strongly to the proposal, mainly on the grounds of cost.

In principle overtime should be occasional, or due to exceptional technical and organisational reasons which cannot be met by the hiring of new workers (Act N. 1079 of 1955). In the seventies most collective agreements began to limit the total amount of overtime (usually to 150 hours per year) and to strictly control the observance of this maximum. But recently collective agreements have given management a certain number of hours of overtime at its disposal which it needs not make known to trade unions.

In Italy, as elsewhere, there has been increasing pressure to make the system more flexible. Emphasis is placed on the need to calculate working time over periods longer than a week, as a matter of common practice and not as an exception. This is in the interest of the enterprise, but also of the employees themselves, to combine their work duties with family needs. So far redistribution of working time on a multiweekly basis (so called annualization) is provided in quite a few collective agreements.

It is equally guaranteed by the same art. 36 of Italian Constitution that 'the worker shall be entitled to a weekly rest and to annual holidays with pay and shall not permitted to renounce these rights'. Consequently all workers have the right to rest one day a week, although Sunday work may be required for technical or public utility reasons (e.g. newspaper firms, hotels, restaurants, transport industry) and is paid with a special increase in the wage rate. Work on Saturdays, in a five-day working week, is generally not considered as holiday work as regards the wage rate applicable. As for the annual holidays, since 1973 most industry-wide collective agreements recognise, in general, four weeks paid vacation per employee. During this period – usually at the beginning – workers receive their regular pay from the employer.

Since the rules granting the right to annual vacations – as well as to Sunday rests – are imperative, all agreements to the contrary are null. But actual work is equally protected by art. 2126 of the civil code, the consequence being that an employee working during these days receives double pay. The reasons why the above mentioned rights are constitutionally protected are twofold. Firstly the employee is supposed to take a rest (on a weekly or annual basis) to recuperate his/her physical and psycological energies. But secondly, case law underlines the need that workers must devote some time to family life (and to social life too). Not surprisingly case law is generous enough in allowing employees who happen to be sick during their annual vacations (and able to make evidence of that, typically when hospitalized) to get an extension from employers. And this is affirmed also in the context of the family function emphasized earlier.[1]

Beyond these rather general provisions which have *additionally* an impact on family life, there are little doubts that part-time is the practice which is frequently adopted by workers to harmonize work and family duties. It should be underlined that in the past part-time work practices were based almost exclusively on provisions which enabled established full-time employees to transfer to part-time working, rather than on the initial recruitment of workers on a part-time basis. Only a few years ago Act N. 863 of 1984 first regulated part-time on a legislative ground.

The Italian part-time statutory system is very simple indeed. Part-timers are defined as those employees 'who are prepared to work for fewer than the normal hours of work laid down in collective agreements or for specific times in the course of the week, month or year'. Part-time employment contracts have to be stipulated in writing (oral arrangements are invalid and, as a consequence, the employee is supposed to have been hired on a full-time basis), describing in detail the work involved and showing the distribution of the working hours with reference to the day, week, month and year. When it comes to assessing pensions, severance pay and

1. See Corte di Cassazione, 24 March 1994, n. 2833, in *Il Sole-24 Ore Guida normativa*, 23 June 1994.

other benefits the periods worked full time and part time must be taken proportionately into account. Naturally a part-timer who incurs an industrial accident or disease in the course of work has a right to disability pension and/or other entitlements on a full, not partial, basis.

Aside from this rather simple legal framework, it is up to collective bargaining to state the number of workers who may be employed part-time as a percentage of full-time workers, the nature of work on which part-time workers may be employed and arrangements with regard to the hours when part-time work may be done.

Also in Italy part-time work is an employment relationship characterized by daily working hours appreciably less than the normal or standard working hours laid down by collective bargaining ('horizontal' part-time) or by working only on certain days, weeks or months of the year ('vertical' part-time). The resultant reduction in pay is not necessarily proportional (it can even be less than proportional). Needless to say, part-time work must be voluntary and not compulsory. Furthermore, part-timers are not allowed to work extra hours, except where collective bargaining provides otherwise. In general collective bargaining states that regular employees have priority over new employees in a switch from full-time to part-time and vice versa.

Part-time clearly fulfils the function of combining work and family duties. Not by chance company-level agreements negotiated before the enactment of the 1984 legislation used to provide for requests of part-time to be accepted by management where a full-timer needed to look after a sick relative (this responsibility being shared on an alternative basis with a wife or husband).

Part-time work has already become fairly common in Italy (Brollo 1991) in recent years, but it cannot yet be considered a traditional part of labour market practice and its use is still marginal compared with that in northern European countries. However the use of part-time in Italy shares some of the characteristics well known in other countries, in particular that female labour tends to dominate and that existing social relationships – the 'woman's duties in the home' and other familiy-related obligations – frequently play an important role in the choice to work on a part time basis. But the big difference to be emphasised is that the request to introduce part-time has come mainly from the trade unions.

In this way the unions have tried to defend jobs and, at the same time, to save sections of the labour market from total exclusion, while building bridges to those on the outside (for example those in the black economy). The unions reflect a widespread demand, in particular from young people, for alternative and less time-consuming forms of employment which permit other activities, in particular further education but also those linked with family life.

On this issue it must be said conclusively that in the public sector not all civil servants have yet acquired any right to work on a part time basis, (secondary scool teachers may to some extent work on that basis), although in many cases it is possible to concentrate most of working hours in the mornings (for instance between 8:OO and 14:OO). This arrangement meets the expectations of those employees (above all women) who in the afternoon may consequently attend to their family activities. A reform of public employment was passed by the Italian Parliament in 1993, with the final aim of making labour laws closer to those characteristic of the private sector (so called 'privatisation' of employment relationships in the public sector), not yet implemented in practice. This reform, when actually applied, would certainly lead towards the introduction of practices already existing in private employment, including part-time arrangements (Rusciano, Zoppoli 1993).

2. TIME OFF FOR PERSONAL/FAMILY REASONS: THE ROLE OF COLLECTIVE BARGAINING

Focusing now more closely on the discipline of leave of absence and time off for family and personal reasons, one may soon realize that the Governement intervention in this area is very limited. One general provision, (originally laid down by Act. N. 2387 of 1937 in favour of white collar workers only) states that employees, not on trial period, are entitled to 15 consecutive days of absence with standard pay in the event of their marriage (the same right being granted to a woman who resigns to get married). These provisions have now been generalized (to blue collars) and improved (e.g. most employees are entitled to paid leave of usually between 15 and 30 days when getting married) via collective bargaining.

Collective agreements (mainly at industry level) normally provide for the possibility of obtaining special leave of absence for personal or family reasons. But the final decision is left to the discretion of the enterprise according to business needs (as is the decision to grant remuneration). Short periods of time off are often granted for these kinds of reasons through custom and practice.

The national collective agreement for insurance companies states that employees have the right to 2 days paid leave in the case of the death of a close relative (child, parent, brother or sister). Moreover, management retains the discretion to grant more time off (paid or unpaid) for personal or family reasons (as an example an employee with more than 3 years service has the right to a maximum of 2 months continuous leave). Bank employees, according to their own collective agreement, have the right to 3 days paid leave in the case of the death of a member of the family or birth of a child and paid time off for medical visits. Moreover the collective agreement states that 'the absences for brief periods of paid leave which the company grants for justified personal or family reasons are not calculable in the annual leave'. It is also stated that 'for family reasons of a private nature, the company may grant adequate periods of leave of absence, determining whether – and for how long – it must pay the employee'.

The national collective agreement for construction workers grants up to one year unpaid leave for private/family reasons (but the company retains the right to check the continuing existence of the reasons, revoking the authorisation in the negative case). Construction/building cooperatives allow employees to take special leaves not exceeding 4 months when they have to look after drug-addicted relatives. Other agreements provide for similar time off arrangements: sometimes employers are authorized to hire a replacement during that period through a fixed-term contract (otherwise rather limited in Italy). In general family leaves are not counted in the annual holidays, but are paid separately. Frequently employers state that seniority rights (e.g. seniority allowance) are not calculated in case of family-related leaves.

Some company level collective agreements state that women workers entitled to benefit of unpaid leaves for family reasons, may get in advance a part of their 'seniority allowance' (normally corresponded when the employment relationships is terminated)[2] provided that in this way the company has not to pay more than half

2. The 'seniority allowance' (*indennitá di anzianitá*) is a payment made by the employer to the employee whenever an open-ended contract of employment is terminated. Act No. 287/1982 has reformed the system of seniority allowance which has been also renamed 'end-of-service allowance' (*trattamento di fine rapporto*). One of the major innovations is the employee's right to get in advance (i.e. before the termination of the contract) part of the allowance under some circumstances provided either by statutory law or collective bargaining.

of the worker's monthly salary. Earlier payment (at least in part) of seniority allowance is granted by some enterprise-level collective agreements also to the employee who must pay University fees for his/er children.

3. FEMALE WORKERS IN ITALIAN LABOUR MARKET

The increasing participation of women is the key element underlying the growth of active population in the European Union. In recent years women have been almost entirely responsible for the expansion of the labour force which has occurred. They have, moreover, transformed its social characteristics. Although in 1991 on average four out of every ten members of the workforce were women across the Union as a whole, there are significant differences between Member States, with the share of women ranging from only a third to almost a half of active population. Italy, together with Luxembourg, Ireland, Greece and Spain, belongs to a group of countries where the share varies between 34% and 37% (Commission of the European Communities 1993).

The incidence of unemployment of women in the labour force in the European Union is significantly higher than among men. In May 1993 the unemployment rate for women averaged over 12% whereas for men it was around 9%. In Belgium, Italy and Greece the rate of unemployment for women at the last count was over twice the rate for men.

Teaching is one of the most important occupations for qualified women, mainly in Portugal, Italy and the United Kindgom. Throughout the European Union the majority of teachers are female in every country, except in the Netherlands. In countries like Italy, falling relative pay levels coincide with women increasing their share of teaching jobs, while lower financial rewards dissuade male graduates from entering the profession. The attraction of these jobs for women may be also explained by the working-time arrangements (working life being basically concentrated in the morning, organized on a part-time-style basis).

The above mentioned situation is characteristic of a more general trend, i.e. the concentration of women professionals into public sector work. Women are more attracted to the applied nature and social value of public sector work, to the greater job security, shorting working time and, no less important, flexible leave arrangements. The public sector is also less discriminatory in its employment practices, such as through the use of open public examinations for recruitment through the successful implementation of positive action programmes. One should not underestimate that the entry of women into these jobs has coincided with falling relative pay levels for the public sector. In addition in countries such as Italy women tend to be more qualified than men entering similar jobs suggesting that they have been unable or unwilling to compete with men on the terms and conditions operating in the private sector.

By 1990 clerical work has become a predominantly female occupation: over 60% of clerical workers in the European Union are women. This represents quite a significant change from the start of the decade when most clerical workers were men in a number of Member States, including Italy. As female participation rates increase so does the rate of feminisation in clerical work. Men held approximately 60% of jobs in the European Union, but women held the majority of service sector jobs in every country.

The large influx of women onto the labour market has not been accompanied by much diversification in the jobs they do. Across the Union, both horizontal and vertical segregation – i.e. in terms of the sectors in which women are concentrated and the kind of work they do within sectors – remains a dominant feature of the structure of female employment. A number of factors seem to combine in this respect to produce a cumulative effect. In particular, the growth in importance of part-time working both reinforces job segregation and, at the same time, has the added effect of differentiating the women involved from other members of the workforce. Where it develops, part-time employment reinforces the concentration of women by confining them to an even more limited number of jobs and professions. This is especially true in services where women are employed part-time work predominantly as cooks, waitresses, cleaners and shop assistant.

In the private sector a significant and growing number of women in the European Union are employed under fixed-term contracts rather than in permanent jobs. A substantial proportion of temporary jobs for women are part-time rather than full-time. In 1991, 36% of women employed in the Union under fixed-term contracts worked part-time (as opposed to 14% of men). In the UK the figure was over 75%, in the Netherlands 66% and in Ireland, Luxembourg and Italy over 50%. Nevertheless, because of the comparatively limited importance of temporary jobs in the former two countries and the high importance of working part-time, only just over 10% of women working part-time in the UK and in the Netherlands were employed on fixed-term contracts. By contrast, in Ireland as well as in Spain almost 40% of part-time jobs for women in 1991 were temporary and in Italy the figure was over 30%.

Although the term 'temporary' covers a wide range of jobs, including some of which the contract extends for several years as well as many seasonal and very short term jobs, substantial numbers of women in the latter two countries in particular (Italy and Spain) would seem to be working under inferior terms of employment. While such jobs may give employers a high degree of operational flexibility, they tend to leave women so employed in a vulnerable position.

To a large extent, women working in temporary jobs do so because they are the only jobs available. In 1991, for the nine Member States of the European Union where the relevant data were available, over 60% of women replying to the question on why they worked in temporary jobs did so because they had been unable to find permanent employment. In Spain the proportion was over 85%, in Ireland and Italy, where fixed-term contracts are also an important element in part-time working, it was over 50%.

There is a connection between activity rates of women and family responsibilities. In 1991 over the European Union as a whole 84% of single women aged 25 to 49 without children were members of the labour force, in the sense that they were either employed or actively looking for work. By contrast, the figure for married women in the same age group without children was only 67%. The difference, however, is far from uniform between Member States. In Italy (as well as in Ireland, in the Netherlands, in Luxembourg and in Denmark) though activity rates were lower for women with children, the difference was less than 10%.

There are various reasons for this difference in labour force participation between single and married women over much of the Union. As well as cultural and social factors, they include the fact that family responsibilities are not confined to bringing up children but extend to caring for a household and carrying out the domestic duties which it entails. It may also be the case that although the comparison relates to married women without children of 15 and under, a proportion of these will have children who are now older than this, who may have been a reason for such women giving up work in the past. The low activity rate, in other words, may partly reflect the difficulty which these women have in returning to the labour market after a period of absence.

Although having one child seems in general to have a relatively minor effect on the participation of women in the labour force, the responsibility of taking care of more than one child, however, does reduce activity rates in most parts of the Union. Activity rates of Italian women with one child was around 47%, falling down to 30% with two.

In contrast with the more visible character of temporary and part-time working, outworking, including homework, has a lower profile in the labour market. Outworking encompasses work at home or outside the employer's or organiser's premises. It can take the form of piecework or the combination of piecework and fixed payments, frequently found in Italy. Intrinsic to outwork, however, is the dependent, subordinate and isolated economic position of the – almost always female – worker, separated from the sale or marketing of her output, be it pottery for tourists or shoes for the fashion market. Italy seems to be the Member State in the European Union with the highest number of homeworkers (minimum estimates: some 700,000) and highest proportion of women (over 90%).

The high proportion of women in homeworking, combined with its suitability for labour intensive industry, serves to reinforce the sex segregation of women. The existence of homeworking – be it legal or in the black economy – has the advantage of offering women the opportunity to become economically active in regions devoid of waged work or where service employment is at yet underdeveloped. However, homeworking is one of the least protected types of employment. In Italy labour law protection exists but, for a variety of reasons, homeworking and homeworkers tend to disappear into the black economy or 'instant selfemployment' at the first sign of regulatory enforcement.

Homeworking is in Italy an example of one of the more unchanging features of the position of women in the labour market. Interestingly it has proved extremely adaptable to contemporary conditions of production. The recruitment of women into homeworking serves as a substitute for capital investment, with the domestic premises of the homeworkers substituting for the costs of factory premises, and reduces the social costs of employing labour.

Family helpers share with homeworkers many similarities in their position on the labour market, despite their concentration in different sectors. The term 'family helper' is generally used to cover three categories of economically active people: (1) wives working in their husbands' enterprise; (2) relatives working in family enterprises; (3) assistants who work with the self-employed without a contract of employment. These forms of no-waged employment constitute a small and diminishing percentage of total employment in the Union, except in three countries: Italy, Spain and Greece where they are important share of women's employment (over 60%). Helping out a husband or a relative in a family business, like accepting irregular homework or seasonal employment in tourism, is a survival strategy for women in the fragmented labour markets of the less developed regions. It has little in common with the situation of full-time family helpers in enterprises of Northern European cities or, for example, the full-time skilled homeworkers in the silk industry of northern Italy.

Some further information may be offered more directly related to Italian labour market. Women's employment and unemployment have been increasing in recent years, an indication of changing attitudes to women seeking a job. Factors in the increasing numbers of women in employment have included higher educational attainment (45% of university degrees were awarded to women in 1989) and demographic trends. Italy's birth rate, at 1.29 children per couple, is below zero population growth.

However, despite these increases, women's participation in the labour force remains low. Out of a total labour force of over 23 million in 1989, only 7,1 million were women. According to OECD statistics, the participation rate for women of working age in 1989 was 44%, one of Europe's lowest, compared with nearly 78% for men. Women's unemployment stood at an average of 16.9% (1,445,000) in 1991 compared to 7.1% (1,059,000) for men.

With regard to the presence of women in the higher echelons of business and public life, the figures are even more disappointing. Only 3.3% of industrial managers are women. In the civil service at national level only 496 out of 6.241 employees in management grades are women (less than 8%). At local level, this can be even more marked: of 52 managers employed by Rome Council, for instance, only three are women. In the political sphere, only around 9,000 or 6.5% of the country's 150,000 local councillors and 2.2% of majors are women.

The rate of part-time employment for women in the European Union ranges from 59% for employed women in the Netherlands down to 8% for employed women in Greece (Italy being around 11%). Family responsibilities are certainly one of the major factors underlying the importance of part-time working among women. A significant proportion of young women in the 25 to 49 age group work part-time: in general a linkage may be established between being married and/or having family responsibilities and part-time working, although in southern European countries this trend is by far less important.

Conclusively the position of women in employment is by no means as elevated as their weight in active population and their part in the growth of the labour force. This difference is also due to the fact that women, far more than men, face the problem of having to reconcile the pursuit of a working career with family responsibilities, including not only caring for children but also taking care of the household and undertaking domestic duties. Partly as a result of this, many women take up part-time work, which tends to restrict the kind of jobs which are open to them and, therefore, makes it difficult, if not impossible, to attain senior positions.

In Italy, however, as in other southern European countries, the development of part-time working has been restricted by legislation or by collective agreements (see above § 1). Here, in many cases, childcare and other support is provided within the extended family – rather by the State or employers – to allow women to take up employment.

4. LEGAL DISCIPLINE ON THE SHARING OF FAMILY AND OCCUPATIONAL RESPONSIBILITIES

The legal protection of women at work dates back to 1950 and it was amended in 1971 (De Cristofaro 1989; Borgogelli 1987). Women may not be fired during pregnancy or during the child's first year unless there has been a just cause, interpreted as serious misconduct on the part of the woman, the closure of the business in which she had been employed, or the expiry of her fixed-term contract. As for an Act of

1963 dismissals are void when it can be shown that they resulted from the employee's marriage.

Paid maternity leave is guaranteed under Act 1204 of 30 December 1971. There is no continuous employment requirement, but the woman must be employed and insured at the beginning of pregnancy. The pregnant employee must abstain from heavy or dangerous jobs (if necessary having the right to be transferred) during the whole period of her pregnancy. She must stop work two months before the (expected date of) birth (three in case of a demanding job or longer in cases of certified sickness) and three months after the birth (compulsory period of rest). This period is counted as actual work as regards seniority, annual vacation, 13th month's salary, etc. A further six months' leave is optional during the child's first year as is unpaid parental leave until the child is three if it is ill.

The woman receives 80% normal earnings during maternity leave paid by social insurance and 30% during optional leave. Industry-wide collective agreements, e.g. banking, insurance, metal workers, usually oblige an employer to pay the difference up to the standard wage. During the child's first year the working mother is also entitled to get two rest periods (one hour each) per day which may be taken consecutively. When the working day is less than six hours only one period is allowed. If the female worker wishes to make use of the feeding room or nursery provided by the employer on the premises, the rest periods are of half an hour each and the women concerned have not the right to leave the place of work.

Parental leave is guaranteed under the already mentioned Act 1204/1971 (for mothers) and Act 903 of 9 December 1977 (for the working spouse if he wishes to substitute the mother or where the children are in the father's sole custody; for adoptive mothers and fathers, also when they have been granted the custody of a child prior to its adoption). The mother or the father may take up to six months' leave during the first year of the child's life. Length of service requirements are unspecified. The parent receives 30% of normal earnings from INPS, the National Institute for Social Security. These rights which apply to both private and public sectors, are extended also to adoptive parents, step-parents and guardians acting in place of parents.

Part-time leave is not allowed, but the woman is also entitled to leave of absence, on production of a medical certificate, during the illness of a child of under three years of age. There is also the right to unpaid leave. Parents have the right to return to their job. Parental leave is treated as holiday leave for the purposes of social security. In the place of working mothers (or fathers) absent from work because of parental leave the employer is entitled to take on staff under fixed-term contract.

Some company-level agreements have improved on the legislative provisions. For instance in some enterprises the already mentioned paid leave in case of children's sickness is extended to both parents (on an alternative basis) up to 6 years. Furthermore on the grounds of well documented reasons unpaid leaves may be granted to parents during the first 5 days of their children's enrollment in a kindergarten or in a nursery school.

Paid maternity leave has been extended to self-employed women, but in this case parental time off is not provided for the working spouse who wishes to substitute the mother.

Regulations existing in Italy in many ways seem to be more favourable to the working mother (or father) than those provided by the European Directive on the protection of pregnant workers adopted on 19 October 1992.

Speaking of the regulations enacted by the European Union authorities, special attention should be given to night work. In Italy night work used to be prohibited for women (as well as for children and young persons), but Act N. 903/1977 reduced the restriction from midnight to 6 a.m. and abolished it altogether for women managers and those working in the first aid department of a firm. The Act allows the prohibition to be lifted or further reduced by collective agreement (subject to communication to labour inspector). The derogation is not valid for pregnant employees up to the seventh month following the birth of her child. After initial reluctance, the number of collective agreements (mainly enterprise-wide) lifting the night-work prohibition for women is on the increase.

In Case 345/89 (Criminal proceedings against Alfred Stoeckel) the European Court of Justice offered a fundamental interpretation of art. 5 of the European Union Directive on equal treatment of men and women as regards access to employment and working conditions. Article 5 states that 'application of the principle of equal treatment with regard to working conditions...means that men and women shall be guaranteed the same conditions without discrimination on grounds of sex'. In its ruling the Court found that art. 5 was 'sufficiently precise to impose on the Member States the obligation not to lay down by legislation the principle that night work by women is prohibited, even if that obligation is subject to exceptions, where night work for men is not prohibited'.

As a consequence of this ruling all Member States of the European Union have denounced the 1948 Convention of the International Labour Organisation placing a general prohibition on night work for women. The ILO has stated that it hopes that the countries which have denounced Convention No. 89 will now rapidly ratify the non discriminatory Convention No. 171. But the Italian Government has not yet revised the principle laid down in the Act No. 903/1977 and has consequently received a formal notification from the European Commission. While employers seem ready to welcome new regulations compatible with the Stoeckel ruling, trade unions are resisting any attempt (successfully, so far) of the Government to amend national legislation in this area (Foglia 1992; Ballestrero 1992).

Actually the Commission has brought infringement proceedings in the European Court of Justice against five Member States – Belgium, France, Greece, Portugal and Italy – on the grounds that they have not amended national legislation on night work to provide for the principle of equal treatment for women and men. Since the Stoeckel judgment, the Commission has been pressing those Member States with legislation banning women's night work to amend it to eliminate the discrimination. Their failure to do so – apparently due in some cases to inability to convince trade unions and employers to reform collectively agreed provisions – has led the Commission bringing proceedings against the five countries on the grounds to fulfil their obligations under the EC Treaty.

It is worth remembering that art. 37 of Italian Constitution states that 'a working woman shall have the same rights and, for equal work, the same remuneration as a male worker. The conditions of work shall be such as to permit her to fulfil her essential family functions, and shall provide special and adequate protection for mother and child'. This consitutional principle has been implemented by the already mentioned Act No. 903/1977 which (art. 1) considers unlawful 'to practise any form of discrimination based on sex as regards access to employment at any level of responsibility, irrespective of the conditions in which the person is recruited and of the sector or branch of activity'. This means that discrimination is prohibited if it is practised by reference to the person's marital status, family circumstances or pregnancy, but also indirectly, through pre-selection procedures or the press or any other form of publicity indicating as an occupational requirement that the person must belong to one or the other sex. This kind of prohibition also applies to any measures taken in connection with vocational guidance, training, further training, insofar as they relate to admission to such facilities or the matters covered by them. Discriminatory practices are also banned as between men and women in connection with the allocation of skills, jobs or promotion.

The statute however does not contain a definition of affirmative action and provides little guidance on the proper implementation of a voluntary programme. Most affirmative action plans which arose from Act No. 903 were results of collective bargaining where female union officials negotiated for the addition of an affirmative action clause in their agreements. Act No. 125 of 10 April 1991 filled many of the voids left open by the previous state, since its aims 'at promoting women's employment and realising a substantial equality between men and women, also through the adoption of positive actions' (Gaeta, Zoppoli 1992; Catalani 1992). Positive actions are defined as those which are 'aimed at removing all obstacles which, in practice, prevent the implementation of equal opportunities' (art. 1, par. 1) and aim at (1) removing inequalities in vocational training and education, access to employment, career development, working life and mobility, (2) favouring a diversification of vocational choice for women, especially through vocational guidance and training, (3) eliminating all working conditions, forms of organisation and distribution of work which have different effects on employees according to gender in terms of vocational training, career development and pay, (4) promoting women's insertion into occupations, activities and grades in which they are currently underrepresented, in particular in high technology sectors and posts with responsibility, and (5) favouring a better balance between family and work responsibilities and a better division of these duties between the two sexes through different working conditions, organisation of work and working time.

The Act provides for the establishment of a special National Committee for the Implementation of Equal Treatment and Equal Opportunities between Men and Women Workers (art. 5). The new Commission is composed of the Minister of Labour (chairperson), five representatives from the most representative trade unions at the national level, five representatives from the most representative employer's bodies, 11 representatives appointed by the most representative women's organisations, one representative from cooperatives, the Equality Councillor (an independent expert appointed by the Government).

The Committee's role (detailed in art. 6) includes the following aspects: (1) to present proposals for the better implementation of the equal opportunities objectives outlined above, (2) to provide information and raise consciousness on the need to promote equal opportunities; (3) to promote the adoption of positive actions by public bodies, (4) to give an opinion (on a qualified majority basis) on the funding of positive action projects, and maintain control of them after their adoption, (5) to draw up codes of conduct of equal treatment, (6) to monitor the implementation of the new legislation, (7) to propose solutions to collective grievances which arise in its field of competence, (8) to require the Labour Inspectorate to gather information from workplaces on the employment situation of the two sexes in terms of recruitment, training and career advancement, and (9) to promote the adequate representation of women on the national and local bodies responsible for vocational training.

The section of the Act No. 125 (art. 4) dealing with the possibility of legal action in cases of discrimination and the sanctions against those discriminating is its most controversial aspect. Importantly, it reverses the burden of proof in discrimination cases. It defines discrimination as any treatment arising from the adoption of criteria which, on a proportional basis, disadvantage workers of one or the other sex, and which refer to requirements which are not essential for work performance. Therefore, for example, public employment examinations and selection procedures must state that vacant posts are open to applicants irrespective of sex.

The onus is on the defendant to prove the absence of discrimination when the claimant provides factual evidence based on statistical details of recruitment practices, pay, work allocation, transfers, promotion, and/or dismissals which indicate the existence of discriminatory practices. The Equality Councillor can initiate legal action if collective discrimination has occurred and it is difficult to identify affected workers. (art. 4, par. 6). A judge can order an employer to introduce a programme designed to remove discrimination following consultations with employee representatives at company level, higher level trade unions and the Equality Councillor (par. 7). During legal investigations, employers will not be eligible to receive the standard relief (fiscalizzazione) from social costs (par. 9) and, if found guilty, they will be ineligible for any form of State assistance, from public tenders to direct aid (par. 10).

Also in Italy the discussion on protection and promotion of women at work has been very lively, since there is now a widespread conviction that some protective measures proved to be counterproductive in the end. For example employers have vehemently opposed and criticized the enactment of Act No 125, arguing that companies will refrain from employing female workers for fear of future legal action and subsequent financial penalties. They claim that the new Act will promote a massive amount of costly and time-consuming litigation. However independent observers contend that the measure is a necessary and belated initiative to give effect to the equality principles of the 1977 Act.

Act No. 125 reflects a preference for collective bargaining as the appropriate method for implementing affirmative action plans, but this requires cooperation between the employers and the unions. At the same time the role of Equality Councillors, as implementors of affirmative actions, should not be underestimated. Although the Equality Councillors have existed previously, they were organised exclusively on a national level. Now they are also established at the level of each region, being responsible to act and implement measures on a more practical level.

A step further in the Governmental policy to strengthen the role of female workers in the labour market was made on 25 February 1992 when Act No. 215 was passed in order to foster basic equality and equal opportunities for men and women in economic and entrepreneurial activities.

The main objective of the Act are the following: (1) to foster the creation and development of female entrepreneurship, particularly in the most innovative fields of the various productive sectors, (2) to promote entrepreneurial training and to further the professionalism of businesswomen, (3) to encourage (also in financial terms) enterprises with predominantly female personnel, and (4) to develop women's knowledge of the running and management of family businesses.

The envisaged benefits of the regulation apply to the following organisations: (a) cooperatives and companies in which at least 60% of the workforce is female, (b) individual enterprises which are managed by women, and (c) enterprises, associations, companies (also those supposed to promote entrepreneurship, with combined public and private funds), training centres and professional associations which promote business training courses or enterprise creation, or consultancy services and technical and managerial support services which are reserved for 70% for women.

Besides such regulations, a national Fund has also been established for the development of female entrepreneurship with a financial allocation of LIT 30 billion for 1992–94, spread evenly over the period. Through the Fund, the first three types of enterprises mentioned above may obtain the following facilities: (a) financing of up to 50% of expenditure for installation and equipment, (b) reimbursement of up to 30% of the costs incurred for the purchase of services which, amongst other things, are intended for increased productivity, for reorganisation, the transfer of technology and the development of quality systems.

The regulation also provides for financial facilities through credit institutions and banks of no more than LIT 300 million for a maximum of 5 years. The interest rate will be 50% of the rate that applies in the sector to which the beneficiary company belongs. The interest rate may be reduced to 40% in relation to the going rate for enterprises which are active in the south of the country.

5. SPECIAL PROVISIONS FOR WORKING PARENTS ASSISTING SERIOUSLY HANDICAPPED CHILDREN

Act No. 104 of 5 February 1992 lays down regulations for the assistance, social integration and rights of handicapped people. Art. 33 provides special rules for working parents who have the responsibility to assist seriously handicapped children (also adoptive ones).

The optional leave granted to parents after the birth during the child's first year (see above § 4) is extended up to 3 years, provided that the handicapped child is not hospitalized on a full-time basis. Or, alternatively, parents may get 2 hours paid time off every working day during the child's first 3 years (art. 33.1,2).

When the handicapped person is over 3 years old, either the working mother or father or a close relative have the right to get 3 days paid leave every month, provided that the handicapped is not hospitalized on a full-time basis (art. 33.3).

More interestingly, parents (or close relatives), when they are employed in the public or private sector, assisting, on a permanent basis, a relative (living together), have the right to choose, when possible, the worksite closest to the place where they live and cannot be transferred to another place of work without their consent (art. 33.5).

The actual implementation of these regulations is a bit controversial. The unions claim that too frequently employers are in practice reluctant to behave according the law.

6. RECONCILING WORKING LIFE AND FAMILY LIFE: CURRENT TRENDS AND FUTURE PERSPECTIVES

Although in Italy there is no general statutory right to paid time off for personal reasons, legislation has at least regulated some aspects of working life to harmonize it with family responsibilities.

So far, however, the Government has proved to be unable to draft any proposal providing for leave to care for elderly relatives: an increasingly important problem due to the the aging of society. Across the European Union the perspectives for the development of the working population's age structure suggest that from about the year 2010 onwards, close to 40% of people will be aged between 45 and 65. Up to the present time the policies implemented have mostly consisted of removing elderly employees from working life. This has produced a number of negative consequences (demotivation of employees remaining in the company, loss of competence, increase in socio-economic costs for society). Research projects carried out at the European Union level recommend to resist the systematic exclusion of ageing workers, with a view to finding a way of keeping employees at work and in good health (European Foundation 1993).

What is clearly lacking in the Italian context is a form of paid perental leave (Grossman 1993). As a recent research project conducted in Denmark has clearly showed (Holt *et al.*, 1992), the overlap in the working-time schedules of parents has a significant impact on their stress level. Those experiencing the highest stress levels are parents who both work full-time in the day.

One should not forget that frequently shop opening hours are in Italy one of the major difficulties in the attempt to reconcile work and family. The local government in the city of Modena (led by a female mayor) has commissioned an investigation into the opening hours of services in the city and the way they fit with the needs of working women as well as other target user-groups such as pensioners. The results (Comune di Modena 1990) provide probably the most detailed 'mapping' of opening hours of the services in Italy. The final report also scrutinizes women's strategies, and the strains involved, in their attempt to fit their working schedules with that of local services. The main conclusion of this survey is that it is necessary that both Government and local authorities intervene to tackle the difficulty of combining working schedules with the inconvenient opening hours of commercial and public services such as shops, schools, nurseries, post offices and doctors' surgeries.

An interesting model in this respect could be the programme launched by the French Government to reconcile work and family, which provides for different kinds of parental leave (e.g. in case of a child with serious illness), already provided by collective bargaining, to be codified into statutory law. Back in June 1986 the European Council approved the Second Community Action Programme on the promotion of equal opportunities for women (1986–1990), which, under the heading 'Sharing of family and occupational responsibilities', stated that member states 'should rapidly adopt the Commission proposal for a Directive on parental leave and leave for family reasons'.

As a matter of fact the proposed European Directive on parental leave never came into force. The proposal was aimed at reassuring, especially young workers, that their professional life could co-exist with their family responsibilities, but also at replacing unofficial practices (e.g. unauthorized absenteeism). According to this proposal 'parental leave' was defined as leave to be granted to working parents during a period after the termination of the mother's maternity leave (but also in case of the adoption of the child), while 'leave for family reasons' was conceived as the entitlement to short periods of leave granted for pressing family reasons to workers with family responsibilities. As regards the key issue of payment during leave periods, the proposed Directive enabled Member States to provide for parental leave allowances payable from public funds, to avoid any need for direct payment by employers which might have a negative influence on the employment of young, temporary replacement workers, etc.

The lack of any statutory provisions on parental leave in Italy may be explained also with the failure at the European Union level to enact a Directive in this field. That did not prevent, however, another Member State, Greece, passing a very interesting act. But Italy also lacks any legal regulation concerning other important practices like career breaks and re-entry schemes, despite the clear suggestions coming from the European Union. And differently from other Member States (e.g. Belgium, the United Kingdom and the Netherlands) collective bargaining provisions in this matter do not exist at all.

Nevertheless it is worth mentioning an experiment conducted at Zanussi, the 'white goods' manufacturing group owned by the Swedish muntinational Electrolux, in the context of its participatory approach to labour-management relations. Zanussi has agreed a 'women-friendly' working time pattern at its Susegana plant where 500 out of 600 employees are women. The project known as 'Operation Rose' involves going from the present individual and imposed condition to a concept of collective, self-managed working hours. Groups of three workers are able to decide which shifts they wish to work, on a weekly or daily basis, within a, 18-hour daily operating time. Surprisingly enough in more than six months no worker has taken advantage of the new mechanism and both management and trade unions are re-considering this project which probably did not meet workers' expectations. This failure also demonstrates that combining work and family responsibilities is a problem to be solved by not necessarily assuming any form of solidarity amongst employees.

So far in Italy the working time issue and arrangements are discussed under the basic initiative of employers (Treu 1988) and flexi-time deals have been concluded at company level mainly for accommodating the special needs of a largely female workforce. But conclusively it seems rather unrealistic to foresee any initiative coming from the Government to amend present legislation. It is more likely that changes could be introduced jointly by the two sides of industry.

REFERENCES

Ballestrero M.V., *Dal divieto del lavoro notturno femminile all autodeterminazione delle donne*, in Rivista giuridica del lavoro, N.4, I, p. 695 et seq., 1992.

Borgogelli F., *Il lavoro femminile tra legge e contrattazione* Milano, 1987.

Brollo M., *Il lavoro subordinato a tempo parziale* 1991

Catalani P., *Eguaglianza di opportunitá e lavoro femminile* Napoli, 1992.

Commission of the European Communities, *Employment in Europe 1993, Report from the Commission*, COM(93) 314 final, 1993.

Comune di Modena, *Le donne nella cittá: tempi, bisogni, servizi* (Cooperative Le Nove, Modena)

De Cristofaro M.L.(ed.)(1989), *Lavoro femminile e pari opportunitá* 1989.

European Foundation for the Improvement of Living and Working Conditions, *Ageing at Work. The European Perspective* Luxembourg, 1993.

Foglia R., *Il divieto di lavoro notturno femminile secondo la sentenza Stoeckel*, in Rivista giuridica del lavoro, N. 4, I, p. 690 et seq., 1992.

Gaeta L., Zoppoli L. (eds.), *Il diditto diseguale. La legge sulle azioni positive* (Torino, 1992.

Grossman D.A., *Voluntary Affirmative Action Plans in Italy and the United States: Differing Notions of Gender Equality*, in Comparative Labour Law Journal, Vol. 14, No. 2, p. 185 et seq., 1993.

Holt H. *et al.*, *Do Working Time Arrangements Affect Stress and Wellbeing in the*

Family?, Danish National Institute of Social Research Copenhagen, 1992.
Ichino P., *L' orario di lavoro e i riposi,* Milano, 1987.
Rusciano M., Zoppoli L (eds.), *L' impiego pubblico nel diritto del lavoro,* Torino, 1993.
Scarponi S., *Riduzione e gestione flessibile del tempo di lavoro,* Milano, 1988.
Treu T., *Italy*, in Blanpain R., Kohler E.(eds.), Legal and Contractual Limitations to Working-Time in European Community Member States (Deventer), p. 324 et seq., 1988.

Japan

Michiyo Kurokawa

1. GENERAL BACKGROUND

1.1. The Characteristics of Employment of Women in Japan

It is important both for men and women to harmonize their working life and family life. In Japan, however, the policy has been discussed with respect to mainly women, though this is beginning to change. It is based on the recognition that women generally have much heavier family responsibilities than men, and in fact, heavy family responsibilities have significant influence on the employment of women in Japan.

(1) 'M-Curve' Employment

The employment rate of Japanese women is 50.7% in 1992 and it has been around 50% for the last 35 years, which is rather high in comparison with other developed countries. Employment by age, however, shows so called 'M-curve' with a bottom (30–34 age group) and two tops (20–24 and 45–49 age groups). It means that many women workers quit their job at childbirth and return after the most demanding period of child care. The 'M-curve' has been a characteristic feature of female employment in Japan, though it is recently shifting upward for due to the increase in employment of the 25–29 age group (because of later marriages) and in middle-aged married women.

The potential employment rate, however, shows a trapezoid, which means that a considerable number of women want to work even during the most demanding period of child-care, if provided with the appropriate conditions.[1]

(2) Working Sectors

As to the working sectors of women, Japan shows a tendency common in many developed countries. According to the study by the General Statistics Bureau in 1992,[2] women tend to be employed in the following sectors: the service sector (31.3%), wholesales, retail and restaurant (27.3%) and manufacturing (25.0%). Recently, the number of women employed in the tertiary sector especially increased due to that sector's recent rapid expansion.

By actual jobs, according to the same study in 1991, many work as clerks (34.9%), in manufacturing (19.5%), as professionals (13.7%) and in sales (12.7%). Those working in administrative jobs are still very few (1.0%) by international

---

1. According to the research on married working women by Association of Women and Youth (Fujin Shonen Kyokai 1989), the necessary factors for women to continue to work are: child care leave (44.2%), leaves for nursing (36.2%), more rest days and annual paid leave (35.1%), flexible working time (32.4%), reemployment system by the previous employer (29.9%), shorter working time (29.4%) and others.
2. General Statistic Bureau, Rodoryoku Chosa (1992) 'Labour Force Survey'.

standards, in spite of the increase in their number that was seen after the enforcement of the Equal Employment Opportunity Law (1985).

(3) Flexible Working Styles

Another feature of female employment as compared to men is their flexible working styles, such as part-time work and worker-dispatching.

Part-time workers have increased since the 1960s, especially since the late 1980s. Women have accounted for approximately 70% of them in the last decade (67% in 1993), and more than 30% of female workers are employed as part-time workers.[3] The majority are middle-aged married women who reenter the labour market after child-care. Therefore approximately 70% choose part-time employment because it is compatible with their family responsibilities.[4]

Worker-dispatching, which was legalized by the Worker-dispatching Law of 1985, is another important working style of women. Dispatched workers increased rapidly since the enforcement of the Law and have amounted to 650,000 in 1992 (about 1.2% of all employees). Compared with part-time workers, they are often young, single women with a higher education, and perform more specified and professional work. According to a study by the Ministry of Labour in 1992.[5] Many dispatched-workers are engaged in operation of office machinery, management of financial affairs and filing. In most cases, they choose this working-style due to its positive aspects that they can decide the job-content and working-time, and that they can use their skills and abilities, rather than due to the difficulty of finding regular employment[6]

(4) Diversification of Women's Preference for Working Life

In recent years, there has been a clear tendency for diversification of preferences for working styles among Japanese women. The working style for women can be classified into 3 categories in accordance with most demanding period of family life; (a) continuation type, (b) reentry type and (c) retirement type. According to the study by the Prime Minister's Office in 1992,[7] an increasing number of women prefer type (b) (68.0%), while those who prefer type (c) tend to decrease (Table 1). Moreover, approximately 30% responded that they would prefer type (a), provided the

Table 1. Women's preference for working styles

	1983	1989	1989*
a) continuation (%)	16.6	14.4	27.2
b) reentry (%)	55.2	64.2	59.3
c) retirement (%)	19.5	17.8	7.6

Source: the Prime Minister's Office, 'Josei No Shugyo Nikansuru Cyosa' (1992).
* = the preference percentage if the appropriate support systems were provided.

3. General Statistic Bureau, Rodoryoku Chosa (1993) 'Labour Force Survey' Part-time worker is defined as those working less than 35 hours per week.
4. Ministry of Labour, White Paper on Labour 1991 (1991, the Japan Institute of Labour), p. 142.
5. The Ministry of Labour, 'Rodosha Haken Jigyo no Heisei 4 Nendo Jigyo Hokoku Shukei', *The collection of reports on worker-dispatching business in 1992.*
6. The Ministry of Labour, *supra* note 4, p. 143.
7. Prime Minister's Office 'Josei no Shugyo ni Kansuru Yoron Chosa' (1992) *Public Opinion Survey on Women's Work.*

appropriate conditions. Further, another study in 1989 shows that many women believe that heavy family life responsibilities such as child-care (58.6%) and nursing of old parents or ailing relatives (48.7%) prevent themselves from working.

1.2. The Long-Term Employment System as the Background

(1) The Long-Term Employment Practice in Japan

In examining Japanese harmonization policies, one cannot ignore the long-term employment system.

There is no unanimous definition for 'Japanese long-term employment practice'. However, it is characterized by its (a) regular recruitment of new school graduates, (b) employment security until the retirement age, (c) flexible personnel deployment such as job-rotations and transfers, (d) intensive inter-firm training through OJT, (e) company unions, and so forth. Established in the 1950s and 1960s, this proctice is still widely accepted in Japanese society as the ideal employment model for regular employees, though employment realities differs by industry and scale of enterprise.[8]

When regarded as a whole, however, the employment system needs a more flexible and peripheral labour force outside the long-term employment practice. These workers, including temporary, part-time and dispatched workers, are distinguished from regular employees in their employment security, wages and other working conditions. The employment of such workers concerns the external rather than the internal labour market.[9]

(2) LEGAL ASPECTS OF THE LONG-TERM EMPLOYMENT PRACTICE

The long-term employment system is legally well founded.

In support of the long-term employment practice, Japanese Courts significantly restrict the employer's freedom to dismiss by so-called 'Doctrine of Abusive Exercise of a Right to Dismiss'. While restricting employer's freedom in this way, it recognizes employer's unilateral prerogative to decide other personnel matters (relocations, transfers and farming-outs etc.) to a considerable extent. There lies the recognition that this kind of personnel deployment is essential to maintain flexibility in the internal labour market under the long-term employment practice.[10]

Moreover, based on the recognition that it has played a key role in keeping the unemployment rate low in Japan, the government's labour market policy has strongly supported the long-term employment practice.[11] Under the Unemployment

---

8. As for the system and its recent development, *see* Takeshi Inagami (ed.), 'Nihonteki Koyo Kanko no Henka to Tenbo', *Modification and Prospects on The Japanese Employment Practice* (1987, Ministry of Finance Press).
9. Yasuo Suwa, 'Japanese Employment Practices and the Law: Brief Comments' in *Management Flexibility in an Era of Changes: The Methods of Accomadating Working Conditions and Work Organizations*, JIL Comparative Labor Law Seminar, pp. 93–100 (1991, The Japan Institute of Labor), p. 94.
10. Y. Suwa, *op. cit.*, pp. 93–94. As for the Court rulings, *see* Kazuo Sugeno, *Japanese Labor Law* (1992, University of Tokyo Press), p. 372 and p. 401ff.
11. As for Japanese labour market policy, *see* Takashi Araki, 'Promotion and Regulation of Job Creation Opportunities' (1994, National Report submitted to 14th World Congress of Labour Law and Social Security, Seoul).

Insurance Law (Art. 61–2), the government grants a large amount of subsidies ('Employment Adjustment Assistance Allowance')[12] to support flexible adjustments in each enterprise to secure employment in case of personnel redundancies. The government also grants similar types of subsidies to support employers' efforts to develop vocational abilities of employees.

(3) Problems Under the 'Long-Term Employment System'

The long-term employment system has surely contributed to the economic success of Japan for the last few decades. However, it poses some problems from the viewpoint of harmonization of working life and family life, which can be categorized in the following way.

1. Difficulties in Harmonizing Working Life and Family Life for Core Workers. The first problem is that core wokers find it difficult to harmonize working life with family life under the long-term employment practice. Some factors which are essential to maintain flexibility in the internal labour market, such as transfers involving a change of residence or overtime work, often present obstacles for women in their pursuit their careers.[13] Moreover, a long leave of absence due to family responsibilities can disadvantageously affect female workers' wage and promotion prospects under the personnel management based on continuous service.

Employers, on the other hand, are often reluctant to hire women as core workers, despite the enactment of the Equal Employment Opportunity Law (hereinafter the EEO Law) of 1985. According to the study by the Ministry of Labour, employers are not interested in the active utilization of women because of a short career expectancy < 46.4% >, necessity to consider their family responsibilities < 9.5% > and a low work consciousness on part of women < 33.1% >.[14]

The separate-track employment system,[15] which was introduced by a growing number of enterprises after the enactment of the EEO Law, is a good example which illustrates how employers compromise with the EEO Law.

The EEO Law requires employers to refrain from discriminating against women in recruitment. The system had been devised to adjust personnel management under the long-term employment practice to the Law. Under the system, employees are channelled into two tracks based on agreements and abilities. One is generally called the 'career track' for core workers in which they have the possibility of promotion to top executive positions, and are supposed to accept company-wide transfers and perform overtime work. The other is the 'general track' which does not involve discretionary tasks and transfers which require a change of one's residence, and with limited possibilities for promotion. The latter track is often provided for women who want to harmonize their working life and family responsibilities.

Under the EEO Law, though employers can not exclude female applicants

---

12. The Employment Adjustment Allowance was introduced in 1974 by a drastic revision of the Employment Insurance Law of 1947, and became the present Employment Adjustment Assistance Allowance in 1977.
13. According to a study by Tokyo Studnet Vocational Center in 1989, female college students tend to prefer assistant work, and those who aim at administrative occupation are one-fifth of that of boy students.
14. The Ministry of Labour, 'Joshi Koyo Kanri Kihon Chosa', *Basic Survey of Female Employment* (1993). For the summary of the survey, *see* 1993, *Japan Labor Bulletin* Vol. 32-No. 8, pp. 2–3.
15. As for the separate-track employment system, *see* Sugeno, *supra* note 10, p. 132ff.

from either track, it is legal to recruit only women for the 'general track' (see below). As a result, few women are recruited for the 'career track', partly due to the employer's discriminatory actions and partly their own reluctance to join the 'career track'.[16]

2. Difficulties in Finding Suitable Jobs in Case of Reentry. The second problem is that, once female workers leave employment for child-care and so forth, it is difficult to find suitable jobs for their abilities and education. Since it is very difficult to return into the workforce as regular and full-time workers, they often reenter the labour market as non-regular workers such as part-time and dispatched workers.

However, as mentioned above, there is a clear gap between regular- and non-regular workers in personnel management. The latter are usually employed as a peripheral and flexible workforce outside the long-term employment practice. The problem is especially serious for part-time workers. Though part-time workers are typically a temporary and menial labour force, the number of 'quasi-part-time workers' have recently been growing. Generally, they have lower wages and working conditions despite job responsibilities,length of service and working hours which are equal to those of regular workers (see below 3.3).[17]

3. Government Policies to Solve the Problem. As discussed below, the government attempts to solve these problems through legislation and administrative measures, and the recent development of policies for harmonization of working life and family life is noticeable.

On the other hand, however, the government is very prudent in taking measures which entail modification of the long-term employment practice, since it is the basic policy of the government to maintain the practice in the future.[18]

2. THE BASIC PHILOSOPHY OF THE POLICIES FOR HARMONIZATION

2.1. Harmonization from the Viewpoint of Equality

(1) The Basic Structure of the Equal Employment Opportunity Law

In Japan, the EEO Law was enacted in 1985 as the fundamental law in the area of equality in employment. Its ultimate goal is to promote the welfare of women workers through < a > promoting equal employment opportunities and < b > assisting the employment of women workers (Art. 1).

For < a >, the Law contains provisions restricting various discriminatory actions against women (Art. 7–Art. 11), which were newly established. For the purpose of < b >, the Law succeeded the Working Women's Welfare Law of 1972 (see below 2.2). This part of the Law contains provisions for the development of vocational

---

16. Ginko Sato, 'Danjo Koyo Kikai Kintoho no Snen', *5 Years After the Enactment of the EEO Law* (1990, Romu Gyosei Kenkyusho), p. 155ff.
17. Ministry og Labour, 'Part-time Rodosha Sogo Jittai Chosa' (1990) *Study on The Actual Working Conditions of Part-time Workers.*
18. In June 1994, Chuki Koyo Vision *Vision on Mid-term Employment* by the Employment Policy Committee was submitted in which it declares that the long-term employment system should be fundamentally preserved in the future.

abilities of women, assistance for reemployment, and support for harmonization of their working life and family life (Art. 22–Art. 28).

(2) The Promotion of Equality Under the EEO Law

The EEO Law has several features which distinguish it from similar legislation in other countries.

1. Mixture of Equality and Protection. The first and most important characteristics of the EEO Law is that it does not make a clear distinction between the principle of equal treatment and protection of women, which can come into conflict.[19] Instead, the EEO Law regards promotion of equal treatment and employment assistance for women as two vehicles for improving the women's welfare. The law's legislative intent is that it is necessary not only to suppress discrimination, but also to give support for women in order to achive the goal. There lies the recognition that women generally receive less favorable treatments in employment and bear heavier family responsibilities than men.

2. Its Unilateral Nature. The ultimate goal being the improvement of welfare of women, the EEO Law is not concerned with discriminatory treatment against men, though such one-sidedness is severely criticized.[20] Therefore, as stated above, it is not a violation of the EEO Law to exclude men from the 'general track' in recruitment under the above-mentioned separate-track employment system, as long as both tracks are open to female applicants.

On the other hand, we should note that the current legislation does not require the public authorities or employers to take affirmative action and other progressive measures to overcome existing job-segregation. It is because the Law does not aim to realize an equal result in working life between men and women, but to improve the welfare of female workers.

3. Reliance on Administrative Measures. Third, the EEO Law is characteristic in its reliance on administrative measures. Since the law prohibits discriminatory treatment against women in vocational training, fringe benefits,and termination of employment, violations will be void and can constitute a tort. On the other hand, as for recruitment, hiring, assignment and promotion, it only sets an 'employer's duty to endeavor', which is not legally sanctioned, but supposed to be realized through administrative measures. This is the result of a compromise with employers who insisted on the difficulties in modifying the current system of personnel management based on the long-term employment practice.[21]

(3) Employment Assistance and Protection for Women

Employment assistance and protection for women in current legislation can be categorized into the following 4 groups;

---

19. This is pointed out and criticized in many articles. For example, *see* Akira Okuyama 'Danjo Koyo Kikai Kintoho no Totatuten', *The Attainments of the EEO Law* (1987, Kikan Rodoho Vol. 144), p. 28ff.

20. Its unilateral nature is severely criticized as being contrary to the principle of equal treatment which essentially includes both sexes, and that it promotes the existing job segregation between men and women. For example, Tadashi Hanami, 'Gendai no Koyo Byodo', *The Present Equality in Employment* (1986, Sanseido), p. 223.

21. Mutsuko Asakura, 'Danjo Koyo Byodo Horon – Igirisu to Nihon', *The Principle of Equal Employment of Men and Women. A Comparison between Great Britain and Japan* (1991, Domesu Press), p. 240.

1. Measures to promote employment opportunities for women by public vocational guidance and training (Art. 22 and Art. 23 of the EEO Law),
2. Protection for maternal functions (pregnancy and childbirth) of women (Art. 65 of the Labour Standards law),
3. Protection for safety and health of women, such as limitation on overtime (Art. 64 Par. 2 of the Labour Standards Law) and ban on night work (Art. 64 Par. 3),
4. Measures to facilitate harmonization of working life and family life, such as a reemployment system (Art. 24 and Art. 25 of the EEO Law) and child care leaves (the Child Care Leave Law).

Under the EEO Law, as stated above, such measures are not contrary to the promotion of equality but necessary. Protection 3 is the exception, however. The government declares that these provisions should be gradually abolished in the future, because they are no longer reasonable and represent obstacles to realizing equal employment opportunities.[22] These provisions were relaxed upon the enactment of the EEO Law, but some have been maintained, in consideration of the fact that in reality women generally bear heavy family burdens.[23]

(4) Policies for Harmonization Under the EEO Law and the Child Care Leave Law

In the current legislation, there are two types of schemes for facilitating harmonization of working life and family life.

One type of scheme is provided only for women under the EEO law. The EEO law requires employers to endeavor to provide reemployment schemes (Art. 25) and, before the enactment of the Child Care Leave Law, to provide child care leaves (Art. 28). These provisions, like some protective statutes under the Labour Standards Law, require employers to treat female workers differently, due to their generally heavy family responsibilities. It is criticized that these provisions can be contrary to the principle of equal treatment under the Treaty on Elimination of Discrimination against Women.[24]

The other type of legislation is the Child Care Leave Law enacted in 1991. The law is based on the idea that family responsibility should be borne by both sexes, and therefore rights to child care leaves should be available for both men and women. The Child Care Leave Law represents a new type of legislation which considers the family responsibility of workers regardless of sex, and this type of law can be enacted for leaves for care of elderly parents in the future (See below 3.2).

2.2. Harmonization from the Viewpoint of Human Resource Management

(1) Japanese Basic Perspective for the Utilization of Female Labour

1. The Working Women's Welfare Law. In Japan, since the 1960s, the era of high

22. In the course of the legislation, employers strongly insisted to abolish such protective measures. *See* Ryoko Akamatsu, 'Shosetu Danjo Koyo Kikai Kinto ho Oyobi Rodo Kijun ho', *The Equal Employment Opportunity Law and the Labour Standard Law* (1990, Josei Shokugyo Zaidan), p. 216ff. Moreover, an adjustment in domestic legislation was needed to ratify the Treaty on Elimination of Discrimination against Women.
23. Some protection has been further lifted by the revision of The Labour Standards Law in April 1994.
24. a. Okuyama, *Supra* Note 19, P. 27.

harmonization of working life and family life should be provided for more effective utilization of female labour. The first legislation which referred to this harmonization was the Working Women's Welfare Law enacted in 1972. The law's main purpose was to promote the reentry of female workers who had passed the most demanding period of childcare to cope with the labour shortage in the high economic growth era.[25] To this end, the law required the State and the prefectures to take action providing vocational guidance, and established the employer's duty to endeavor to grant conveniences for pregnancy, childbirth and childcare. In 1985, the Working Women's Welfare Law was revised and absorbed into the EEO law.

2. The Basic Idea of the Present Labour Market Policy. For the past two decades, utilization of female labour has become an increasingly more important issue in Japanese labour market policy, since it is regarded as a key to cope with recent changes in the labour market: the long-term labour shortage due to the rapid aging of population and low fertility rate on the supply side, and the growing needs for flexible and highly-skilled labour due to technical developments and expansion of the service sector on the demand side.[26]

The essence of the present policy is that various working styles should be prepared for women so that they can make choices to harmonize their working life and family life. The government repeatedly declares that the public policy should aim to prepare an environment in which women can make a prefered choice, while harmonizing their working life and family life.[27]

(2) Promotion of Flexibility in Working Life at Various Levels

Based on the recognition, the government takes measures to promote flexibility of working life at various levels. There are several types of approaches for the harmonization in the current legislation.

First, the Worker Dispatching Law (1985) and the Part-time Workers Law (1993) provide flexible working styles which are compatible with family responsibilities. These schemes reconcile both women's preferences for 'reentry type' of working style, and employers' demand for a temporary or flexible labour force.

Second, the Child Care Leave Law (1991) supports smooth continuation of employment during demanding period of family life, by promoting flexibility in working life through a career break system. They are based on the recognition that, under the long-term employment practice, interruption of employment have high costs for both workers and employers from the viewpoint of human resource management. The government has recently established the Guidelines on leaves for care of elderly parents (see below).

Third, reduction in working time and flexible working schedules can facilitate harmonization, though it will not be discussed further here. In Japan, flexible working schedules such as flex-time systems were introduced by the revision of the Labour Standards Law in 1987. A 40-hour work-week system was also introduced

25. M. Asakura, *supra* note 21, p. 195.
26. As for recent developments in the Japanese labour market, *see* Atsushi Seike, 'Recent Employment Situation and the Long-term Structural Change' (1994, *Japan Labor Bulletin* Vol. 33-No. 1), p. 4ff.
27. For example, *see* 'Dainiji Joshi Rodosha Fukusi Taisaku Kihon Hosin', *The Second Basic Plan on Measures to Promote the Welfare of Female Workers*, which was established in 1992 under article 6 of the EEO Law.

by this revision, but it was enforced step by step through administrative guidelines.[28] In 1993, the overall annual working hours were 1,912 hours, which was considerably shorter than before but still longer than many European countries and the United States.

2.3. Harmonization from the Viewpoint of Demographic Change

Recent demographic changes have had a strong impact on the policies for harmonization in Japan. In other words, it is a driving force behind the recent policy development. In 1990, the fertility rate in Japan had declined to 1.57 which was the lowest level in Postwar period (so-called 1.57 shock). The government feared that this would aggravate the long-term labour shortage and the financing of social security for the growing number of senior citizens. One of the reasons for the low fertility rate was thought to be the difficulty for workers (especially women) to harmonize working life with family life. The Child care leave law (1991) was then enacted as a countermeasure.[29]

On the other hand, in Japan, the number of senior citizens are increasing rapidly and it is estimated that the number of elderly people over 65 will reach 32 million or 23.6% of the population in the year of 2020. It is already becoming a heavy burden for workers (especially women) to care for frail elderly parents. According to a study in 1989,[30] nearly 40% of workers who are engaged in such nursing are forced to leave their employment or change working conditions significantly. Therefore, the government has come to realize that schemes to facilitate such care are necessary. In 1990, it started a campaign for employer awareness, and in July 1992, established the Guideline on Leaves for Nursing.

3. THE PRESENT LEGAL SYSTEM FOR THE HARMONIZATION IN JAPAN

3.1. Assistance for Reemployment of Female Workers

The EEO Law provides some measures for the reemployment of women who left employment by reason of pregnancy, childbirth and child-care. The aim of these provisions is to increase employment opportunities for such women, for under the long-term employment system in Japan, it is rather difficult to return to employment on a regular and full-time basis.[31]

The law requires the State to give considerations to establish and coordinate measures for vocational guidance, job placement and vocational training to facilitate reemployment (Art. 24). Article 25 Par.1 also establishes the duty for employers to endeavor to 'take special measures for reemployment' for such women.[32]Based on Art. 62 Par.1 of the Unemployment Insurance Law (1976), the State pays 'Women's

---

28. As for the revision in 1987, *see* Sugeno, *supra* note 10, p. 207ff.
29. Tatsuko Fujii, 'Ikuji Kyugyo ho Seitei no Haikei to Sono Gaiyo', *The Legislation of the Child Care Leave Law and its Context* (1992, Kikan Rodoho, Vol. 163, pp. 29–44), p. 34.
30. Koyo Shokugyo Sogo Kenkyusho Chosa (1989) *Study by the General Research Institute of Employment and Occupations.*
31. K. Sugeno, *supra* note 10, p. 306.
32. 'Special measures for reemployment' means, for example, to give priority to such workers in recruitment.

Re-employment Promotion Subsidy' to employers take special reemployment measures.

3.2. Career Break System for Child Care and Care for Elderly Parents[33]

(1) The Child Care Leave Law

As mentioned above, the Child Care Leave Law (1991) represents a new type of legislation that extends the scope of application to male workers, compared with the EEO Law which limits its scope solely to women. Moreover, it substituted a legal right of employees for the employer's previous obligation to endeavor to grant child care leaves under the EEO Law (Art. 28).

The goal of the law is to improve worker's welfare through facilitating smooth continuation of employment of workers caring for their children (Art. 1). This is especially significant for regular employees under the long-term employment practice, though the Law covers some part of non-regular employees as well.

1. The Right to Child-Care Leaves. The Labour Standards Law guarantees the right of maternal leave for women 6 weeks before and for 8 weeks after childbirth (Art. 65).[34] Moreover, the law prohibits dismissals during the leave (Art. 19 Par.1). The Child Care Leave law gives workers the right to child-care leaves if the child is less than 1 year old. However, the law does not apply to workers employed on a fixed-term basis (Art. 2). The employer cannot refuse requests for leave unless there is a written agreement prescribing the cases in which the employers can refuse the request. Such an agreement should be reached with a union that organizes a majority of workers in the undertaking, or a representative of a majority of such workers. Those who can be denied the request by the agreement are (a) workers with less than 1 year of service, (b) workers whose spouse can fully care for the child and (c) workers to whom employers have a reasonable ground for refusal which is to be clarified in the enforcement ordnance (Art. 3).[35]

Child care leave can continue until the child becomes 1 year old, and the employer should specify the period at the worker's request (Art. 6).

A discharge because of a request for or taking of a child care leave is prohibited (Art. 7). Though the law does not provide regulations concerning wages and working conditions during and after a child care leave, it stipulates that the employer should endeavor to clarify them in advance (Art. 8). Moreover, the government promulgates guidelines for the contents of the measures to be taken by employers (Art. 12–1). The guideline mentions that workers should not be treated unfavorably for their taking a child care leave (item 2).

2. Other Measures. The law sets forth employer's obligations to endeavor to take other measures to supplement child-care leaves. First, the law requires reductions or other working hours arrangements, for workers with a child under 1 year old who do not take child-care leaves (Art. 10). As to a worker with a child between 1 and the

---

33. For General Information, *See* Ryuichi Yamakawa 'recent Developments Regarding Child and Elder Care Leave in Japan' (1994, *Japan Labor Bulletin* Vol. 33-no.10, Pp. 5–9).
34. Maternal leaves after childbirth is compulsory and must be granted regardless of whether it was requested by the worker. It was extended from 6 weeks to 8 weeks by the revision in 1985.
35. For example, workers who work less than 2 days a week can be excluded by the agreement (item 3–2 of the enforcing regulation).

age entering elementary school, the employer should endeavor to take measures similar to the above (Art. 11).

Second, employers are required to endeavor to be flexible in personnel management so that the employees can freely take child care leaves. The law also requires employers to endeavor to take measures to maintain and develop vocational abilities of the employees during their child care leaves to facilitate their smooth return (Art. 9).

The contents of such measures are further clarified in the guidelines mentioned above.

3. The Right to Child-Care Allowance during the Employee's Absence. When the Law was enforced, child care leave was without pay unless otherwise agreed upon by the parties.[36] However, the 'Childcare allowance' has been introduced by a revision of the Unemployment Insurance Law in June of 1994.[37] Under the revised law, the 'Childcare allowance' belongs to the 'Employment-continuation allowance' which has been newly instituted as a part of the unemployment benefit program. The 'Employment-continuation allowance' is based on the idea that unemployment benefit should be provided not only when the employment of an insured person is interrupted, but also when there exists obstacles such as childcare that impede the smooth continuation of employment. The expense is financed by premiums paid by employers (50%) and insured employees (50%). Under the program, 25% of the previous wage is paid to workers during a childcare leave.

(2) Leaves for Care of Elderly and Sick Relatives

There is no legislation for leaves of this nature in Japan. In July 1992, however, the government established 'the Guideline on Leaves for Nursing'. It is based on the report by the 'Committee for A Study on Guidelines for Leaves for Nursing' in 1991. Consideration of current trends, the report concluded that it was too early to guarantee a leagal right to such leaves for workers through legislation, and that the system should be diffused through administrative guidance and guidelines.

Based on inquiries to enterprises which have already introduced the system, the guideline shows the standard of the schemes which employers should provide for facilitating harmonization of working life and family life of workers who are engaged in nursing of family members (item 1).

According to the guideline, a system of nursing leaves is necessary to prevent worker's involuntary retirement because of emergency needs for nursing of family members (item 2). Such system should be available both for men and women, and at least for 3 months per person who requires care. The leave should be granted at least when his or her spouse, children, parents or parents-in-law need such care. The guideline states that it is inappropriate to grant the leave only when no one else can nurse the person in place of that worker (item 3). The parties should decide wages and other working conditions during and after the leave, and employers should not prevent workers from taking leaves through disadvantageous treatment.

---

36. According to Ministry of Labour, White Paper on Labour 1994 (1994, Japan Institute of Labor), p. 256, 32.3% of the companies provide some compensation for their employees during child care leaves.

37. As for the revision, *see* Chuo Shokugyo Antei Singikai Senmon Chosa in 'Koyo Hken Bukai Hokokusho', *Report by the Employment Insurance Devision of the Central Employment Security Committee*. The law was revised based on this report.

The guideline also encourages employers to introduce reduced or flexible working time for such workers (item 4).

(3) The Present Situation
Child care leaves have rapidly diffused after the enactment of the Child Care Leave Law. According to the study by the Ministry of Labour, in October 1992, 50.8% of private companies have the system in place and 48.1% of women with a child have utilized it. However, the percentage varies with company size (Table 2).[38]

Leaves for nursing are also beginning to spread, but the percentage is still low (16.3% in average). The government is now considering legislation for further diffusion of the schemes.[39]

Table 2. Diffusion of the system of childcare leaves and leaves for nursing

Size of company	Childcare leaves (%)	Leaves for nursing (%)
500 workers–	95.2	51.9
100–499 workers	72.2	22.5
30–99 workers	45.1	14.2

Source: Ministry of Labour 'Joso Koyo Kanri Kihon Cyosa' (1993).

3.3. Improvement of Flexibility of Working Styles

In contrast with the career break system mentioned above, some legislation provides alternatives to the working life under the long-term employment practice. The Worker-Dispatching Law and the Part-time Workers Law are important in providing flexible working styles which are compatible with family life.

(1) The Worker-Dispatching Law[40]
In Japan, worker-dispatching had been banned by the Employment Security Law as an illegal labour supply business. In early 1980s, however, worker-dispatching businesses expanded rapidly due to (a) an increase in demand for workers with technical and professional skills because of rapid technical progress and computerization, (b) companies' needs to contract out certain work to slim down their workforce and (c) diversification in the preference for working styles especially among women.[41]

The Worker-Dispatching Law enacted in 1985 legalized the dispatching of workers. It was based on the consideration that worker-dispatching played an important role in providing employment opportunities for women and older workers who often have difficulties in finding suitable jobs for their abilities and educations under the long-term employment practice.

To clarify legal responsibilities of the dispatching agency and the client company, the law defines legal workers-dispatching as 'causing a worker or workers

38. Ministry of Labour 'Josi Koyo Kanri Kihon Cyosa' (1993) *Basic Research on the Employment Management of Women*.
39. The Ministry of Labour, *supra* note 36, p. 257ff.
40. As for the Worker-Dispatching Law and Its Characteristics, *See* Takashi Araki 'charasteristics of Regulations on Dispatched Work (Temporary Work) in Japan' (1994, *Japan Labor Bulletin* Vol. 33-no.5, p. 5ff.).
41. Akira Takanashi, 'Korekara no Koyo Seisaku no Kityo', *The Basic Tone of the Future Employment Policy* (1993, Japan Institute of Labour), p. 119.

employed by one person to be engaged in work for another person under the direction of the latter, while maintaining their employment relationship with former' (Art. 2 Par.1).[42] Therefore, under the Law, dispatched work is a triangular relationship in which a dispatched-worker is employed by a dispatching agency, but is subject to the direction of a client agency. In principle, the dispatching agency is responsible as the employer under the labour protective laws, though some provisions (for example, those on working hours and regulations on health and safety) are also applied to the client company.

The Law is unique, from a comparative perspective, in limiting the sectors in which worker-dispatching may be conducted. Works which (a) requires special techniques, skills or experiences and (b) are considered to require special employment management because of the nature of working styles (Art. 4 Par.1). Under these principles, 16 occupations have been designated by the Cabinet Order.[43] The legislative intent was to prevent worker-dispatching from eroding the job market of regular employees under the long-term employment practice.[44] As a result, dispatched workers tend to be technically skilled professionals; therefore, the Law so far has not had the impact of mobilizing the internal labour market and to changing the long-term employment practice.

(2) The Part-Time Workers Law[45]

The recent increase in part-time work reflects the employers' interests in developing flexible labour, and workers' preference for flexible working styles. Considering the long-term labour shortage in the aging society, part-time work is predicted to become an increasingly important working style for both women and elder people in the near future.[46] For many women, part-time work provides the most favorable working style to balance their working life and family life. However, part-time workers are often employed as unskilled labour not suited to their abilities and education, though recently their occupations have tended to expand and length of service prolonged.[47] Moreover, there is a distinct incongruity between part-time workers and full-time, regular workers in wages, employment securities, and other working conditions.

To remedy this problem, the Part-time Workers Law was enacted in June 1993. The law aims to promote the welfare of part-time workers by (a) improving personnel management of part-time workers,[48] and (b) promoting development of their vocational abilities (Art. 1). Schemes under (a) include an employer's obligation

---

42. K. Sugeno, *supra* note 10, p. 165.
43. They are (1) electric calculator design, (2) machinery design and drafting, (3) machinery operation for producing sounds and images for broadcasting programs, (4) performance in broadcasting programs, (5) operation of office machinery, (6) interpretation,translation and shorthand, (7) secretarial work, (8) filing, (9) market research, (10) management of financial affairs, (11) the drafting of foreign exchange documents, (12) the presentation and explanation of manufactured goods, (13) tour conducting, (14) cleaning, (15) repair of building equipment and (16) building receptionist and guide.
44. K. Sugeno, *supra* note 10, p. 166ff., A. Takanashi, *supra* note 41, p. 118.
45. For an Outline of the Part-Time Workers Law, *See* Yuichiro Mizumachi, 'part-Time Rodo Ho no Keii to Kadai' *Legislation of the Part-Time Workers Law and Its Role*, (1993, Monthly Journal of the Japan Institute of Labour, Vol. 403, Pp. 30–45).
46. Research Group on Part-time work, 'Kongo no Part-time Rodo Taisaku no Arikata ni Tuite', *On the Future Policies for Part-time Work* (1992).
47. *See*, Nobuko Matsubara, 'Tanjikan Rodosha no Koyo Kanri no Kaizen Tou ni Kansuru Horitu', *A Commentary to the Part-time Workers Law* (1994, Romugyosei Kenkyusho), pp. 13–40.
48. The law defines 'short-time worker' as those whose working time per week is shorter than that of regular workers who are employed in the same undertaking (Art. 2).

to endeavor to give workers a document to clarifying the working conditions (Art. 6), to hear opinions of the representative of a majority of part-time workers (Art. 7) and to appoint a person responsible for personnel management of part-time workers (Art. 9). Other schemes can be provided by the guidelines of the government (Art. 8). As for (b), the law requires the State,the prefecture and the Employment Corporation to give consideration to part-time workers for vocational training, and endeavor to fill up job placement (Art. 11–12). Furthermore, the Short-time Labour Assistance Center, which provides services such as information, counseling and training projects for part-time workers is established under the Law (Art. 13–Art. 30).

The law does not declare the principle of equal treatment for part-time workers and full-time workers. Instead, it attempts to solve the problem by imposing the 'employer's obligation to endeavor' which would be realized through administrative guidance. In other words, the law adopts soft gradual methods, similar to the EEO Law, to avoid drastically changing personnel management under the long-term employment practice.[49]

4. CONCLUSION: CHARACTERISTICS OF POLICIES FOR HARMONIZATION IN JAPAN

(1) Japanese Perspective on Equality and Support for Harmonization

The first and most important feature of Japanese legislation is that it allows and even encourages differencial treatment of women and men, consideration of the general disadvantages in working life, especially heavier family responsibilities.

The EEO Law is not concerned with discriminatory treatment against male workers. Therefore, it is completely legal for employers to provide measures which facilitate harmonization of working life and family life solely for female workers. Moreover, the Law requires employers to take such measures and aids the employers' efforts through subsidies and other forms of support.

This character of the EEO Law comes from a lack of a clear distinction between the principle of equal treatment and protection of women. Under the EEO Law, it is not contrary to the promotion of equality to provide assistance and protection for women, at least in context of the present circumstances where women generally bear heavier family responsibilities than men. Instead, the law is based on the idea that both types of measures are necessary to realize equal opportunities in the present Japanese labour market.

Recently, however, the Child Care Leave Law of 1991 appeared as a new type of legislation in this field. Compared with the previous provision in the EEO Law which required employers to provide child care leaves solely for women, the new law guarantees a right to leaves for both sexes. The Law is based on the idea that schemes for harmonization of working life and family life should be provided for workers with an child regardless of sex, as stated in The Treaty on Elimination of Discrimination against Women (Art. 11 Par. 2(c)). This type of law may be also legislated for leaves for the care of elderly parents in the near future.

(2) Japanese Pattern of Policies to Realize Harmonization

Second, it should be noted that the government does not aim to realize equal results in

---

49. Y. Mizumachi, *supra* note 45, p. 32.

Second, it should be noted that the government does not aim to realize equal results in working life by facilitating the harmonization. Instead of eliminating the existing differences between men and women, Japanese labour market policy aims to enable women to make a choice while balancing their working life and family life, through promoting flexibility in working life at various levels. These policies are also supported from the perspective of human resource management, since there is a growing need for flexible and skilled labour to cope with the present and future change in the labour market.

The present legislation can be categorized into three groups. The first is the Worker-Dispatching Law and the Part-time Workers Law which provide flexible working styles that are compatible with family responsibility. They aim to provide suitable jobs for especially female workers reentering the labour market. The second is the Child Care Leave Law and the Guideline on Leaves for Nursing, which facilitate the smooth continuation of employment by promoting flexibility in careers. The last are the measures for reduction and flexible schedule of working hours, which were introduced by the revision of the Labour Standards Law.

(3) Japanese Method to Enforce the Policies for Harmonization

Third, Japanese policy for harmonization can be characterized by its reliance on administrative measures.

As for matters in which various interests of workers and management are involved, legislators often avoid precise stipulations in the law. Instead, the laws often set 'employer's obligation to endeavor' and leave it to the administrative guidance based on guidelines, while assisting labour-management efforts and providing subsidies. The EEO Law and the Part-time Workers Law are typical examples of such legislation. The Child Care Leave Law, which guarantee the right to child care leave, also has this character (for example, the provision on wages and working conditions during and after leaves).

These 'soft' enforcing measures come from the legislative intent that the interests of the labour market parties should be considered and the law should not be devorced from actual situation.

Moreover, schemes for harmonization often have the effect of modifying the personnel management for both regular and non-regular workers, and can lead to a significant modification of the long-term employment system itself. We can see the trend of Japanese labour market policy which has been strongly supported by the long-term employment practice as the background for these enforcing measures.

APPENDIX 1
MINISTRY OF LABOUR, WHITE PAPER ON LABOUR 1991

PART II. PRESENT STATE AND PROBLEMS OF FEMALE AND YOUNG WORKERS

Chapter 1 Background of Problems concerning Female and Young Workers

Section 1 The Relation between Changes in Attitudes toward Working and Recent Demand and Supply of Labour Market

Women's participation in the labour market seems to be due to women's growing desire to work In recent years, however, the proportion of those who 'are ready to work' in those who want to work has been declining. An increasing number of women are employed as part-timers as well as full-time workers. Hence, women's diversify ing attitudes toward working should be considered.

Figure 24. Comparison of attitudes toward work and leisure between generations (males).

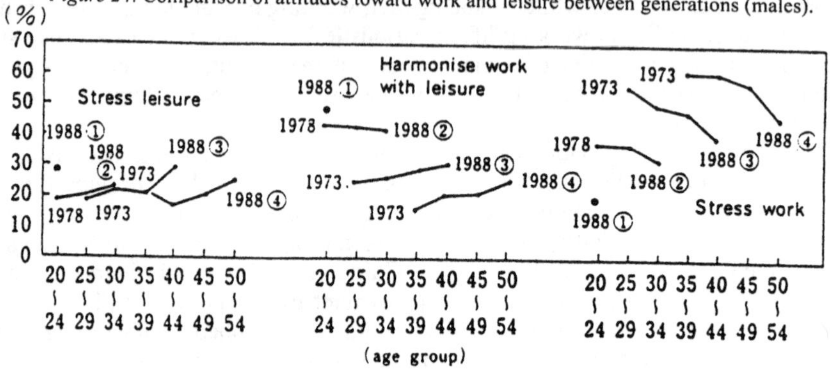

Source: NHK Public Opinion Research Division. *Japanese Value Orientation*
Notes:

1) Five possible choices for reply are provided to the question on work and leisure: a) 'Find something to live for in leisure rather than in work', b) 'Finish the work promptly to enjoy leisure as much as possible', c) 'Stress both work and leisure', d) 'Enjoy leisure occasionally but will concentrate one's energy on work' and e) 'Go all out to find something in work'.

Those who selected a) and b) of the five choices are categorized into 'Stress leisure'', those who selected c) into 'Harmonize work with leisure' and those who selected e) and e) into 'Stress work'.

2) In this chart, figures for the years for those of the same generation are linked together to see changes by the passage of time and to facilitate a comparison between generations.

① denotes those who were in the 20–24 age group in 1988

② denotes those who were in the 20–24 age group in 1978 and in the 30–34 age group in 1988 (10 years older than those in ①)

③ denotes those who were in the 25–29 age group in 1973 and in the 40–44 age group in 1988 (20 years older than those in ②)

④ denotes those who were in the 35–39 age group in 1973 and in the 50–54 age group in 1983 (30 years older than those in ①)

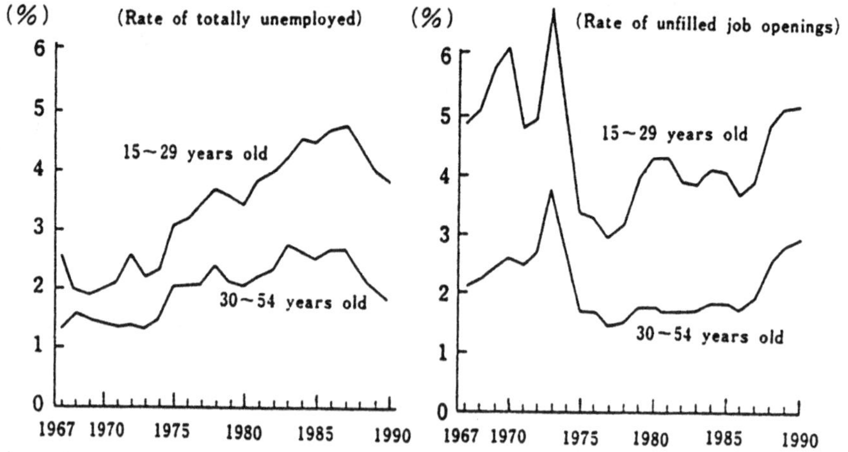

Figure 25. Levels of and trends in rate of totally unemployed and rate of unfilled job openings (for those falling under ages from 15–29 to 30–54).
Source: Ministry of Labour, *Report on Employment Service,* Statistics Bureau, Management and Coordination Agency, *Labour Force Survey*

Notes:
1) Rate of totally unemployed and rate of unfilled job openings were both obtained on an employee basis. For instance, rate of totally unemployed/(no. of employees workers + no. of totally unemployed) and was represented in percentage.
2) The rate of unfilled job openings was obtained by: no. of unfilled job openings/(no. of employees + no. of unfilled job openings)
The number of unfilled job openings by age was obtained by distributing the annual average number of unfilled job openings by the age-wise composition of unfilled job openings to regular workers for October.
Unfilled job openings are obtained by excluding the number of placements from that of active openings.

Some of consciousness on occupation and labour differs among people of different age, and a large part of this difference is affected by the difference among generations. Taking an example of the question. 'Which is more valuable for your life, job or leisure?' The younger the answerers, the fewer prefer 'job', the more prefer 'try to make both compatible'. Observing respective generations by applying the Cohort comparison method, it is found that differences among generations considerably affect those among the ages (Fig. 24).

Unemployment rate of the young showed a long-term upward trend, while fluctuating in immediate response to business fluctuation, and demand for young workers was stronger. These changes did not come suddenly in recent years; but they gradually became prominent, it seems, with youths' changing attitudes toward working (Fig. 25).

Section 2. Changes in Employment Structure and Labour Supply and Demand

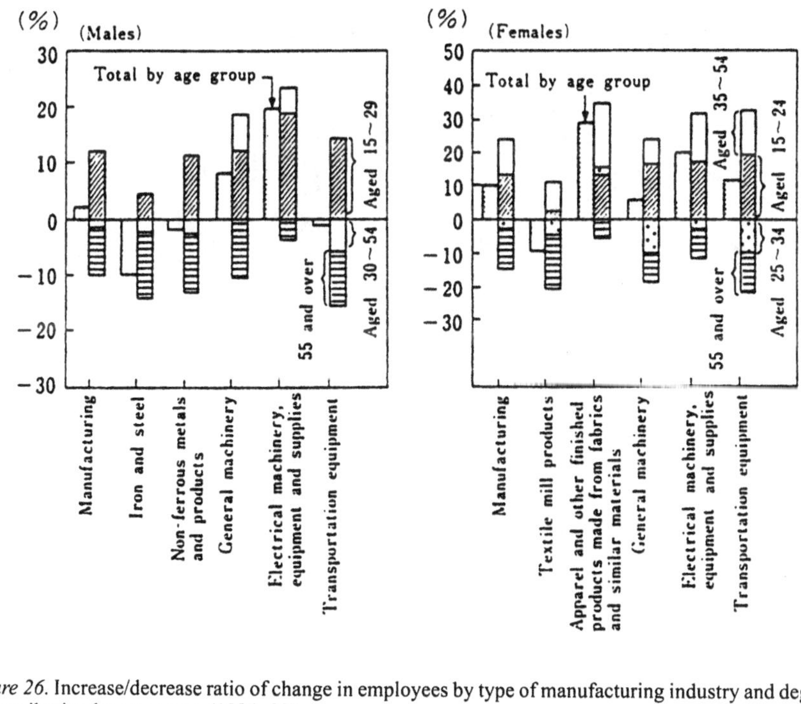

Figure 26. Increase/decrease ratio of change in employees by type of manufacturing industry and degree of contribution by age group (1984–89).

Source: Ministry of Labour, *Surveys on Employment Trends*
Note: Degree of contribution by age group is calculated by finding balances between 1984 and 1989 within the same generation. For instance, the degree of contribution of employees in the 30–54 age bracket is found

by subtracting the number of those in the 25–49 age bracket 5 years ago (or in 1984).

Women and the youth seem to have contributed greatly to the adaptation of Japan's economy to changing environment. As we will see below, they have assumed a significantly large role in changes in industrial structure as well. Women, for instance, have been a positive factor contributing to the marked increase in the number of employees in such industries as wholesale and retail trade, eating and drinking places, services, and also in electrical machinery, equipment and supplies in the manufacturing sector. In electrical machinery, equipment and supplies, for example, employees showed 20.3 percent growth between 1984 and 1989 – of which women accounted for 9.3 percent.

Look at the rate of employees growth by business category in manufacturing in 1984–89, the rate indicates a high increase in electrical machinery, equipment and supplies and other machinery-related businesses. Because the generation in the "period of entering and reentering the labour market," during which the labour force participation rate rises, moved into businesses with growing labour demand, and this worked considerably in favor of employees growth (Fig. 26). The roles played by female and young workers in the changing industrial and employment structure were so large as to relieve the nation of depending much on middle aged workers for its structural changes.

Observing the future prospect of young workers, the ratio of the youth labour force of 15-to-24 to the total labour force will again begin to shrink in the year 2000 and will drop below 20 percent in 2010. Also, the number of youth labour force is predicted to dip below the current level (Fig. 27).

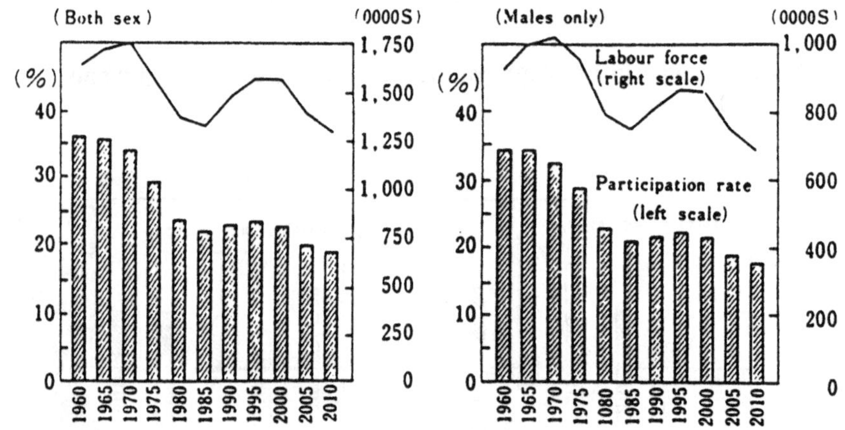

Figure 27. The labour force aged 15–29 and the proportion in total by age group (Trends and Projections).

Source: Statistic Bureau, Management and Coordination Agency, *Labour Force Survey, A Report by* "Study Group of Employment Vision for Long-Life Society"
Note: Values for 1995 and beyond are estimated by the above report.

Chapter 2 Women's Entrance into the Labour Market and Their Diversified Working Lives

Section 1 Realities of Employment and Female Workers

Features of Supply Structure of Female Labour Force and its Changes. In Japan, the pattern of female labour force participation rate by age group describes an M-shaped curve – a "dip" in the age group corresponding to the period of childbirth and childcare and a "rise" in the subsequent groups. Such a tendency is not observed in major Western countries (Fig. 28).

The female labour force participation rate has shown steady rise. By age group, the rate shows overall upward shift and it has a sharp rise particularly in the 25-to-29 age group. Consequently, the bottom in the "M" has shifted from the 25-to-29 to the 30-to-34 age group (Fig. 29).

Let us classify factors behind the rise in the female labour force participation rate of 25-to-29

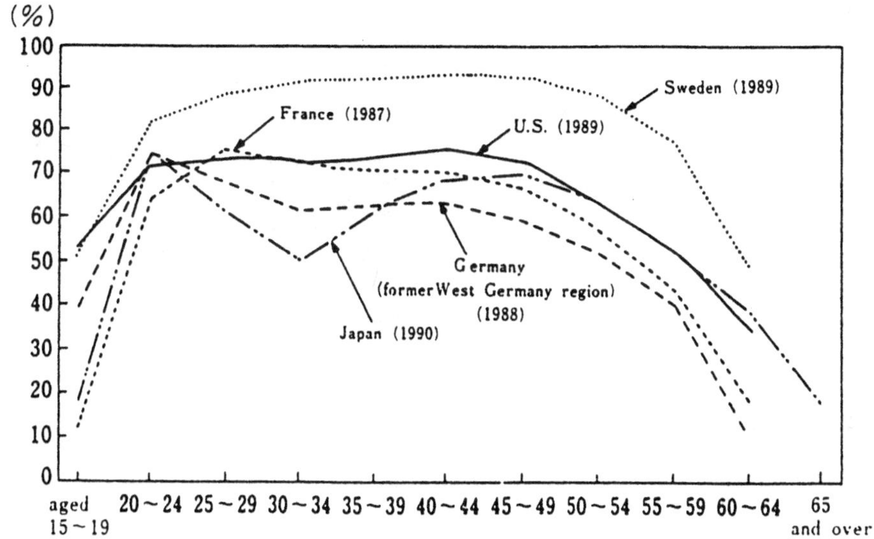

Figure 28. International comparison of female labour force participation rate.

Source: ILO, *Year Book of Labour Statistics*

age group into the three different categories: a rise in the rate for single women, a rise in the rate for married women and changes in population constitution by marital status (effect of marriage at higher ages) resulting from increasing ratio of single women with the higher labour force participation rate than married women. In 1980–85 and 1985–90, the changes in population constitution or women's tendency to marry in later years, affected to a greater degree than the rise in the labour force participation rate for

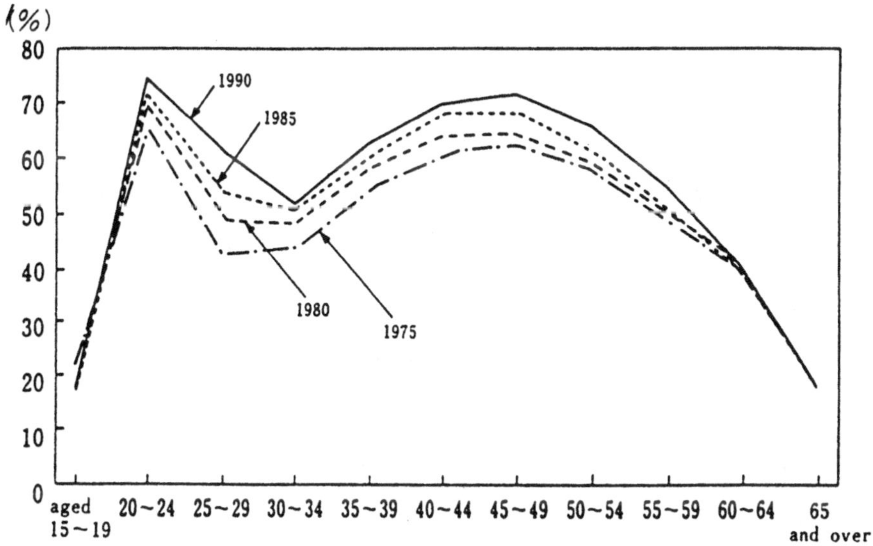

Figure 29. Trends in female labour force participation rate by age.

Source: Statistic Bureau, *Labour Force Survey*

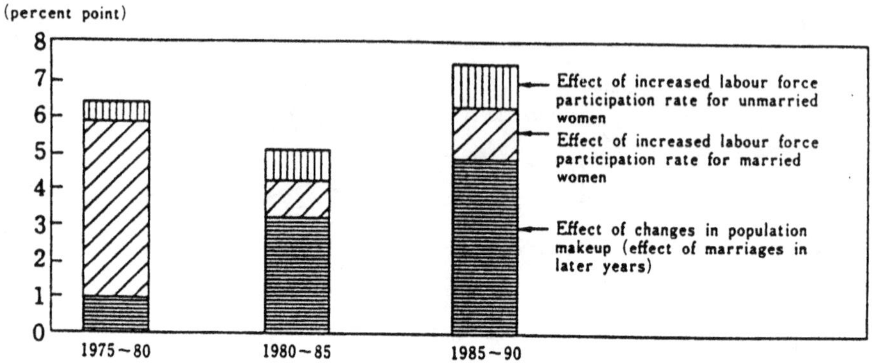

Figure 30. Analysis of factors behind changes in female labour force participation rate for those in 25–29 age group.

Source: Statistic Bureau, Management and Coordination Agency, *Labour Force Survey.*
Note: 1) Factors are analyzed by:

$$\alpha = \frac{\Sigma\, Ni\alpha i}{N}$$

$$\Delta\alpha = \underbrace{\frac{\Sigma\left(Ni + \frac{\Delta Ni}{2}\right)\Delta\alpha i}{N + \Delta N}} + \underbrace{\frac{\Sigma Ni\left(\alpha i + \frac{\Delta\alpha i}{2}\right) - \Delta N\cdot\alpha}{N + \Delta N}}$$

Effect of changes in labour force participation rate — Effect of changes in population make up (Effect of marriages in later years)

N: Population aged 25–29.
L: Labour force participation rate for those aged 25–29.
(Subscript i represents marital status).

2) The effect of changes in the population make up by marital status due to the increase in the proportion of unmarried women with a higher labour force participation rate than that of married women.

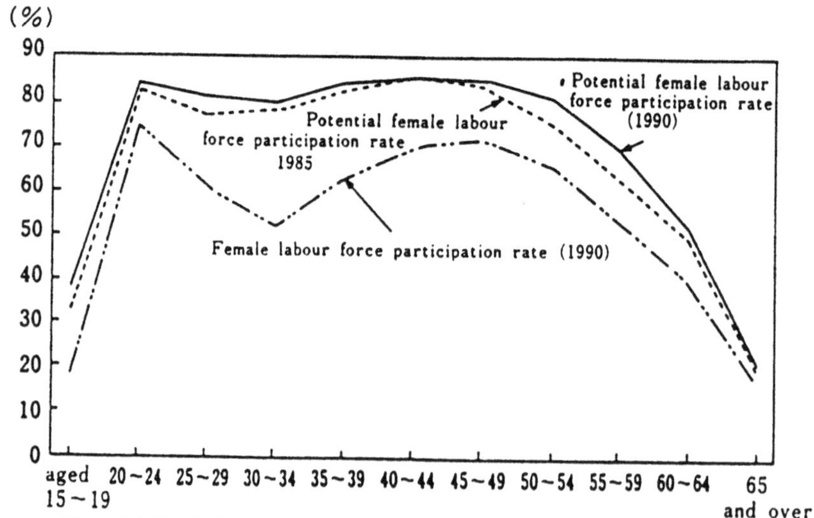

Figure 31. Trends in potential female labour force participation rate by age group.

Source: Statistic Bureau, Management and Coordination Agency, *Labour Force Survey, Special Survey of the Labour Force Survey* (Special Tabulation)
Note: Potential female labour force participation rate by age group

$$= \frac{\text{Female labour force (by age group)} + \text{women wanting to work (by age group)}}{\text{Female population 15 years old and over (by age group)}} \times 100$$

both single and married women (Fig. 30).

The number of women who are not in labour force and want to work increased by 290,000 for five years from 7.55 million in 1985 to 7.85 million in 1990. Looking at the proportion of the so-called potential labour force (labour force and above-mentioned women wanting to work) to the population by age group, or the potential labour force participation rate, the M-shaped curve, which is described in the pattern of (actual) labour force participation rate by age group, loses its shape. This means that women in the age group, in which many leave the labour market due to childbirth and childcare, have a strong desire to be employed (Fig. 31).

Of those women who are not in labour force and wish to work, the number of those who said "are ready to work" dropped from 830,000 in 1985 to 600,000 in 1990. In addition, the percentage of such women in all that wish to work has shrunk. This downward trend is shown in all the age groups from the 15-to-19 to the 55-to-59 (Fig. 32).

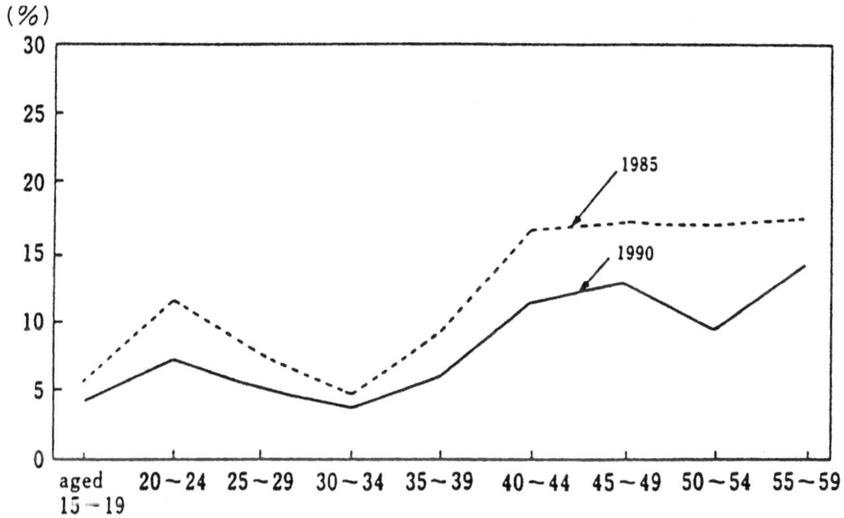

Figure 32. Proportion of those who "are ready to work" in all women want to work.

Source: Statistic Bureau, Management and Coordination Agency, *Special Survey of the Labour Force Survey* (Special Tabulation).

Realities of Employment of Women Workers

Although the ratio of female employees tend to be higher in specific business, such as services, wholesale and retail trade, eating and drinking places, and manufacturing industries, the ratio is rising in many industries. By occupation the ratio tend to be higher in specific occupation such as clerical and related workers, craftsmen and production process workers, professional and technical workers, sales workers, but it is surging in many occupations (Fig. 33).

Observing the educational attainment of female workers by occupation, the rate of higher education level is particularly increasing in the occupations such as clerical and related workers, professional and technical workers (Fig. 34).

Observing the occupation of female workers by age group, in the 25-to-29 age group a proportion of clerical and related workers is highest and the rate of professional and technical workers is

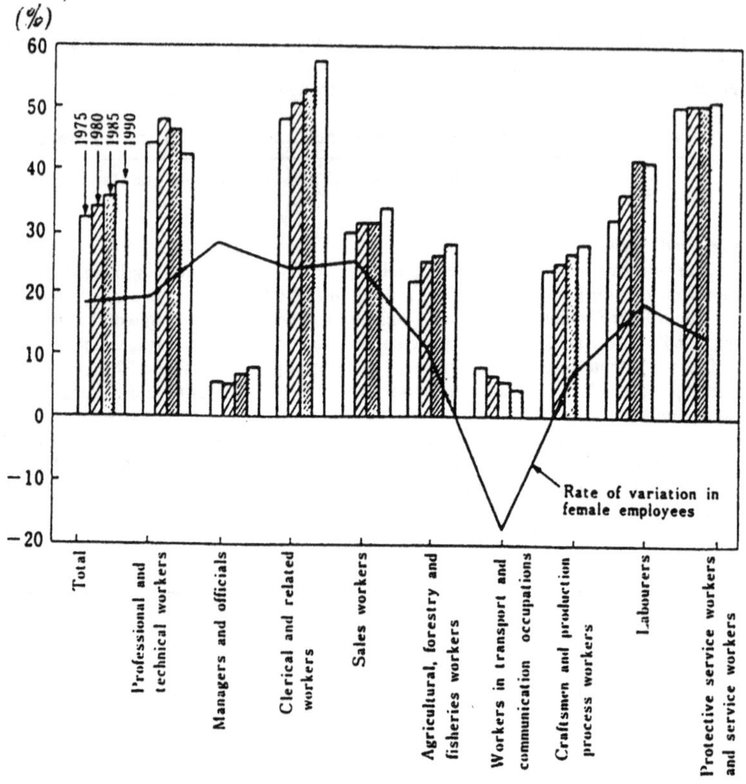

Figure 33. Ratio of women in employees by occupation.

Source: Statistical Bureau, Management and Coordination Agency, *Labour Force Survey*

Note: Proportion of women by occupation = $\frac{\text{Female employees}}{\text{Employees}} \times 100$

Rate of variation in female employees is for the 1985–90 period.

secondly high. However, the ratios of above-mentioned occupations are lower in the age group after 35, in which many women seem to reenter the labour market after childcare, while, the proportion of sales workers, craftsmen and production process workers is increasing (Fig. 35).

Looking at form of employment of women by age group, more women in their late 30s and beyond – many of whom, it is assumed, have reappeared in the labour market after short breaks of childcare – work as part-time workers (short-time employees) than those in the preceding age groups (Fig. 36).

Section 2 Employment Opportunities and Working Conditions for Female Workers

Progress in Equal Opportunities and Treatment between the Sexes in Employment

An international comparison of the ratio of female workers by occupation shows that Japan enjoys a high ratio of female workers in some occupations, such as craftsmen and product process workers. On the other hand, the ratio of female workers who are technical workers, managers and officials is considerably lower in Japan than in advanced Western nations (Fig. 37).

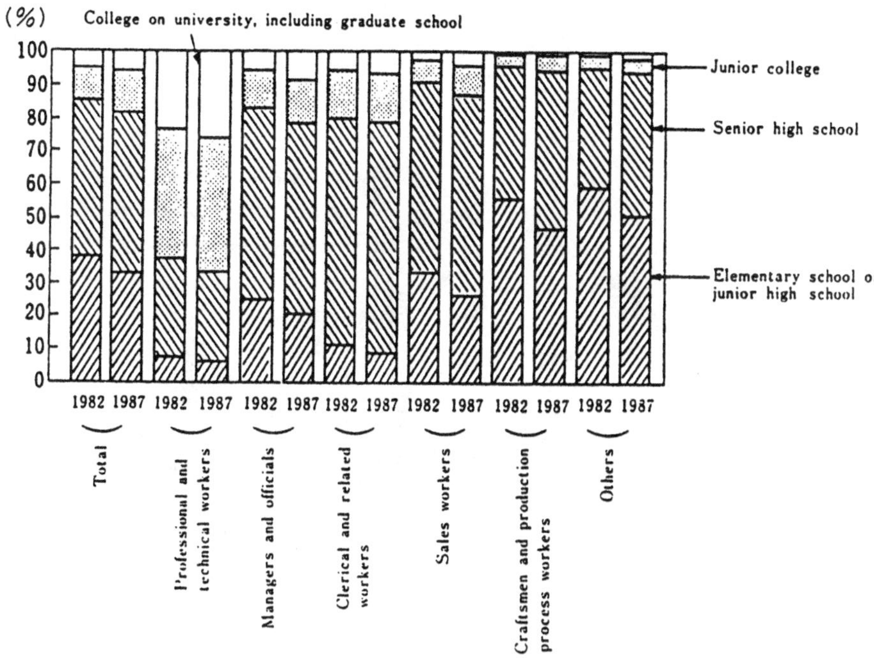

Figure 34. Composition ratio of working women by education–occupation.

Source: Statistics Bureau, Management and Coordination Agency, *Employment Status Survey* (1982, 1987)

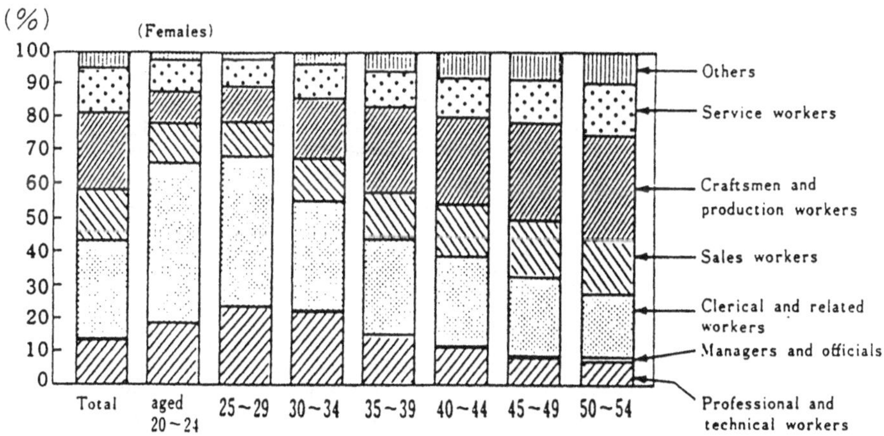

Figure 35. Composition ratio of employed persons by age-occupation (1990).

Source: Statistics Bureau, Management and Coordination Agency, *Labour Force Survey*
Notes:
1) Excludes agricultural, forestry and fisheries workers.
2)Service workers represent "protective service workers" excluding protective service and domestic service workers. In the *Labour Force Survey,* they are classified as "other workers."

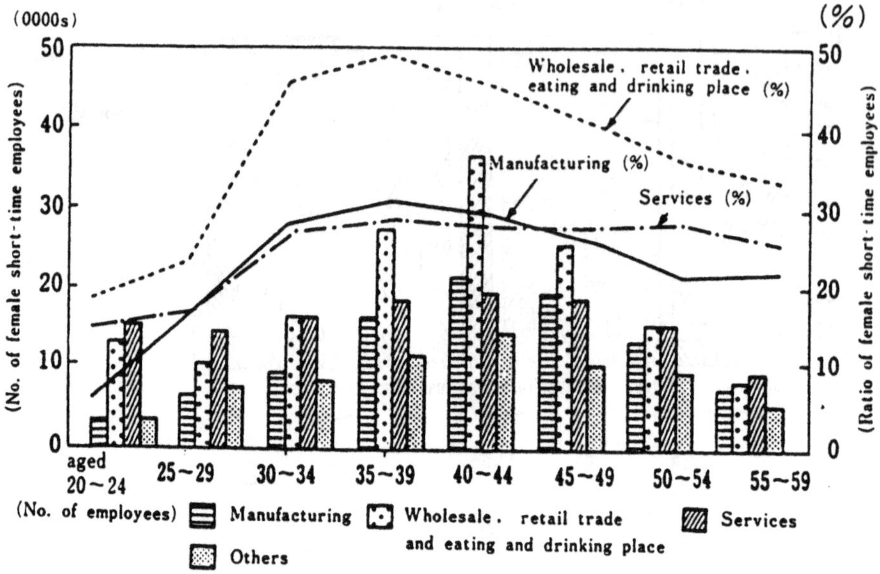

Figure 36. No. of female short-time employees by age group and proportion of female short-time employees (1990).

Source: Statistic Bureau, Management and Coordination Agency, *Special Survey of the Labour Force Survey* (Special tabulation)
Note: Short time means less than 35-working hours a week. Ratio of short time female employees

$$= \frac{\text{No. of short time female employees}}{\text{No. of female employees}} \times 100$$

Regarding recruitment of college or university new graduates, fewer enterprises recruited male graduates alone in 1989 than in 1984 before the Equal Employment Opportunity Law (EEOL) was implemented. Meanwhile, more enterprises recruited both male and female graduates than in 1984. Thus, equal treatment in terms of recruitment has progressed to a considerable degree; some enterprises, however, still recruit men alone. It is thus expected that further improvements will be made (Fig. 38).

Looking at a relationship between the corporate basic concept of assignment of female workers and occupations in which women are engaged, women tend to be assigned to specific occupations, such as clerical and related workers in the enterprises which put women in positions of auxiliary nature alone (Fig. 39). What is more, the corporate basic concept of assignment of women also affects women's promotion.

The EEOL provides provisions for equal opportunity and treatment between the sexes in terms of employment management ranging from recruitment, hiring, assignment, promotion, education and training, fringe benefits, mandatory retirement system, retirement and to dismissal. When compared before and after the enforcement of the EEOL, all these aspects of employment management have largely been improved (Table 40).

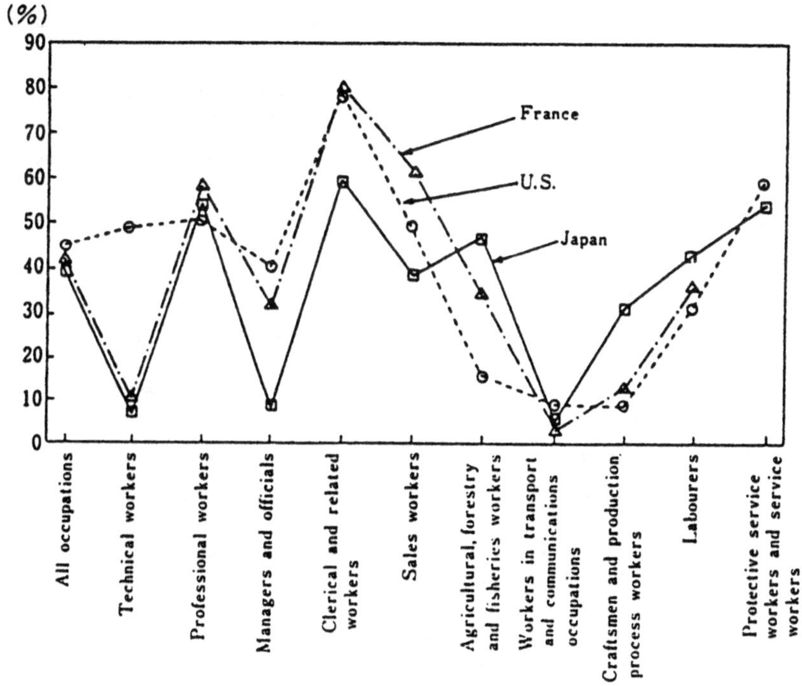

Figure 37. International comparison of ratio of women by occupation.

Source: Statistic Bureau, Management and Coordination Agency, *Labour Force Survey* (1990)
U.S. Department of Labour, *Employment and Earnings* (1990)
France Institut National de la Statistique et des Etudes Economiques, *Enquête sur l'emploi* (1989)

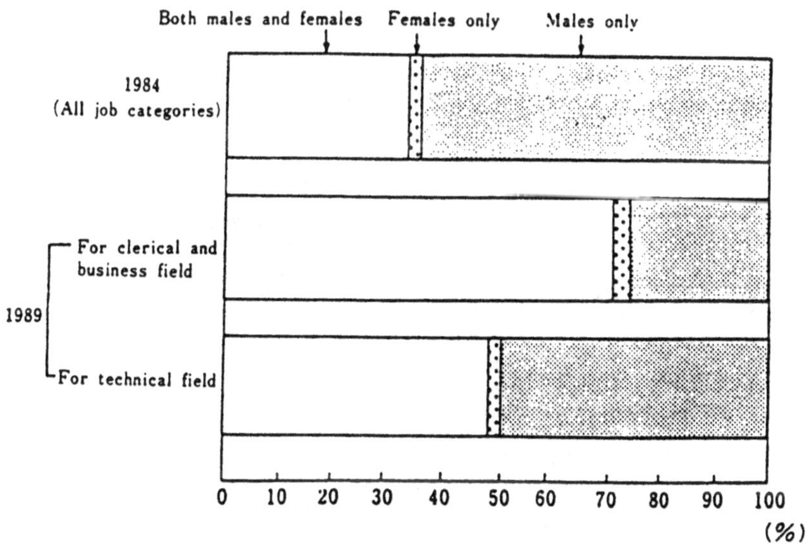

Figure 38. Rate of enterprises by recruitment of new college graduates (industry total).

Source: Ministry of Labour, *Survey on the Employment of Women Workers* (1984), *Survey on Women Workers Employment Management* (1989)

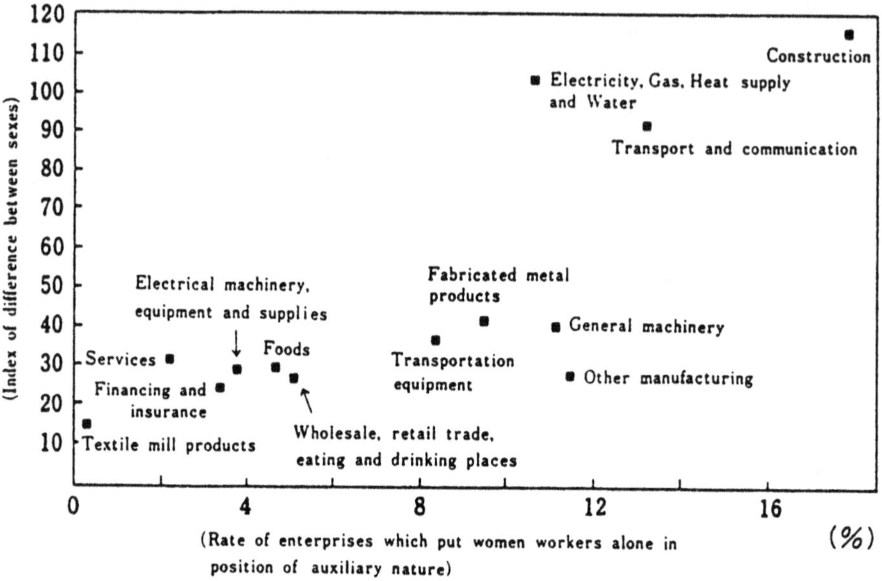

Figure 39. Correlation of industry-wise jobs of auxiliary nature and index of difference between sexes.

Source: Ministry of Labour, *Survey on Women Workers Employment Management* (1989), Statistics Bureau, Management and Coordination Agency, *Labour Force Survey* (1989)
Notes:
1) A correlation coefficient is 0.88.
2) Index of difference between sexes (IS) is calculated as follows. If the ratio of male and female employed workers in each industry (occupation) to those in all industry (occupation) is "t", the ratio of female employed workers in each industry (occupation) to those in all industry (occupation) is "f" and the t for the latest year is "t_0",

$$IS = \Sigma \frac{t_0}{t} \times | t-f | \times 100$$

IS becomes 0 (minimum value) if the composition ratio of sex-wise workers by industry is, exactly the same, while it becomes 200 (maximum value) if it is completely different.

Factors Affecting a Gap in Wages between the Sexes and Their Changes

A gap in wages between the sexes is much affected by that in attributes of workers between them. When matching the composition of female workers with that of male workers to make a fair comparison, a gap in the scheduled earnings between men and women was 68.6 percent after adjustment of the worker composition by position, 68.4 percent after adjustment by year of service and 63.4 percent after adjustment educational attainment, as opposed to 60.2 percent before adjustment (Fig. 41). In addition, the gap was 61.6 percent after adjustment by prefecture. It was 71.9 percent after adjustment by occupation although only specific types of occupations were available data-wise.

Suppose that all the factors that can be adjusted, such as age, educational attainment, enterprise size, year of service and position, are eliminated from the differences in the male and female workers composition. Then a gap in the scheduled earnings will be 62.8 percent after adjustment by age, as opposed to 60.2 percent before adjustment. Furthermore, it was 69.2 percent after adjustment by educational attainment, 71.3 percent after adjustment by enterprise size, 75.9 percent after adjustment by year of service and 78.3 percent after adjustment according to position. Thus, the wage differentials between the sexes narrow to a considerable degree by the adjustment of the workers makeup (Fig. 42). If failure to adjust the worker composition by occupation and inability to classify positions into small segments were taken into consideration, it seems that the differences in the workers makeup could account for much of the wage disparity between the sexes by simple comparison.

Table 40. Improvements for equal treatment after enforcement of EEOL item improvements

Recruitment and hiring	In 1984, 33.6% of enterprises surveyed recruited both male and female new university graduates, but in 1989 70.4% recruited new college graduates for clerical business field while 47.8% recruited them for technical field.
Assignment and promotion	The ratio of female workers in managerial position (above chief clerk) with male and female workers in management positions as 100, has increased. The ratio was 7.4 in 1980, 9.0 in 1985 and 11.5 in 1989.
Education and training	In 1989, approximately 90% of establishments had a training program for both male and female workers. Of them, 97.6% provided training of newly employed for male and female.
Fringe benefits	In 1986, a little over 80% of enterprises surveyed treated both male and female employees equally in terms of a housing loan scheme, a company insurance subsidy plan and aproperty accumulation savings subsidy plan. In 1989, 98.8% treated the sexes equally in terms of fringe benefits. Also, 42.9% equally allowed both male and female workers to occupy domitory in 1986, but in 1989 82.8% did so. However, due partly to the fact that only a few years have elapsed since prohibition of discriminatory treatment between the sexes in 1989, this area has been tardy in making improvements.
Mandatory retirement, recruitment and dismissal	In 1986, 15.0% of enterprises extended the age limit of mandatory retirement system for female workers. When those enterprises which had implemented the same age limit of mandatory retirement system for both male and female workers are included, 97.1% did so. In 1989, 2.5% maintained age limits which differed between men and women. In 1986, 96.5% said that "they had no system which required female employees to quit work upon marriage, pregnancy and childbirth" or that "they had eased such requirements." While in 1989, 1.3% implemented the above-mentioned system.

Source: Ministry of Labour, *Survey on the Employment of Women Workers* (1984, 1986), *The Voluntary Self-Check Comparison* (1989)
Note: The 1984 and 1986 surveys were conducted among enterprises and the 1989 survey, among establishments.

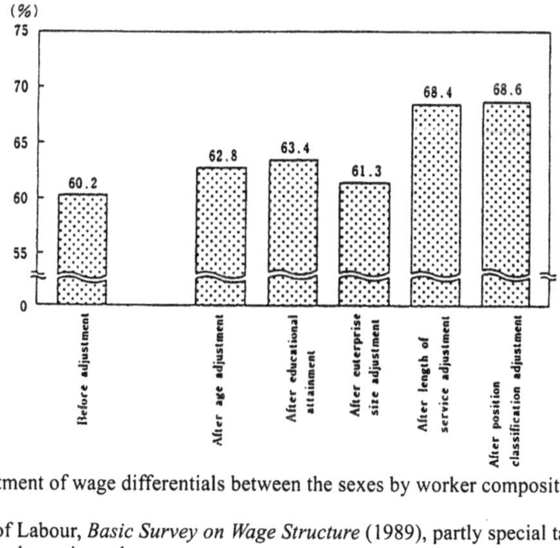

Figure 41. Adjustment of wage differentials between the sexes by worker composition (non-crossed).

Source: Ministry of Labour, *Basic Survey on Wage Structure* (1989), partly special tabulation
Note: Scheduled cash earnings alone.

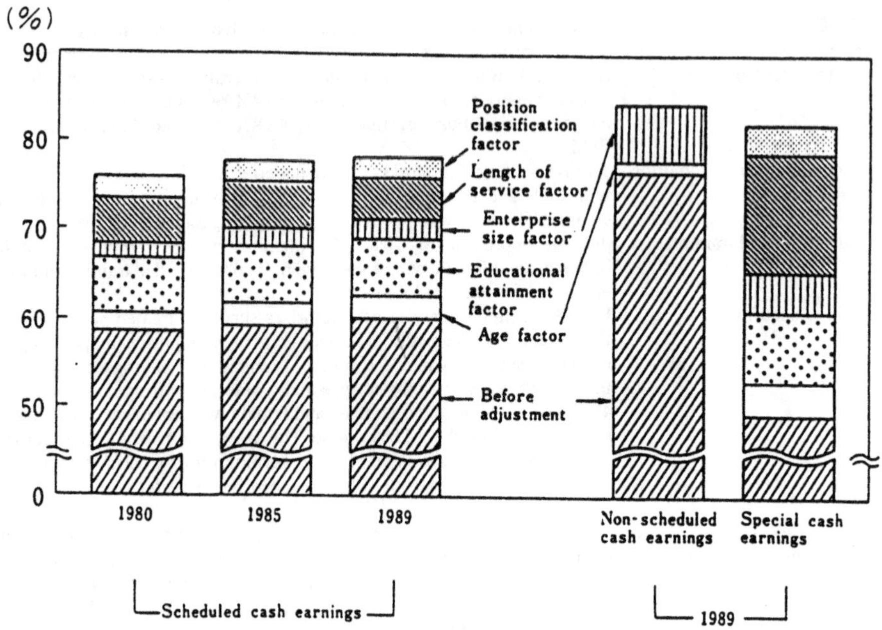

Figure 42. Adjustment of wage differentials between the sexes by worker composition (crossed).

Source: Ministry of Labour, *Basic Survey on Wage Structure* (Special tabulation)
Notes:
1) Here, the wage differentials is adjusted by adjusting the female workers composition by age, education attainment, enterprise size, length of service, position to male workers composition and is indicated in the adjustment process order.
2) Non-scheduled earnings per hour are not adjusted according to length of service and position
3) There are correlations between the factors in the difference in worker composition between the sexes. Any effects from this are included in those factors adjusted earlier.

Section 3 Female Workers' Attitudes towards Working and Lives

Women's Attitudes Towards Working and Their Changes

In Japan there has been the traditional sex-based division of work: "men should work outside, women inside." A comparison of 1987 and 1990 polls on the traditional belief found that the percentage of those who support the belief decreased for both sexes and that of those who do not support rose. However, over a third of the male answerers favored the belief, suggesting the need for further revolution in consciousness (Fig. 43).

The employment pattern working women generally consider most desirable throughout their lives is "reemployment" pattern. The highest, or 64.2 percent of women surveyed said they would quit work upon marriage and return to their jobs only after short breaks, followed by those who opt for "continued employment," or fail to stop working at all, and those who choose to "stay home," or quit work upon marriage to be housewives (Fig. 44).

Looking at the desirable employment pattern for female workers on condition that "systematized maternity and childcare leave and complete childcare facilities are provided," 27.2 percent opted for "continued employment." Meanwhile, a fewer wished to quit work upon marriage. This trend was observed among women in any age groups. By educational attainment it was notable among women of college and university graduates (Fig. 44).

Many female workers cite childcare and care of old parents as reasons for making it difficult for them to continue their work. Thus, it is clear that women at large consider them an impediment to

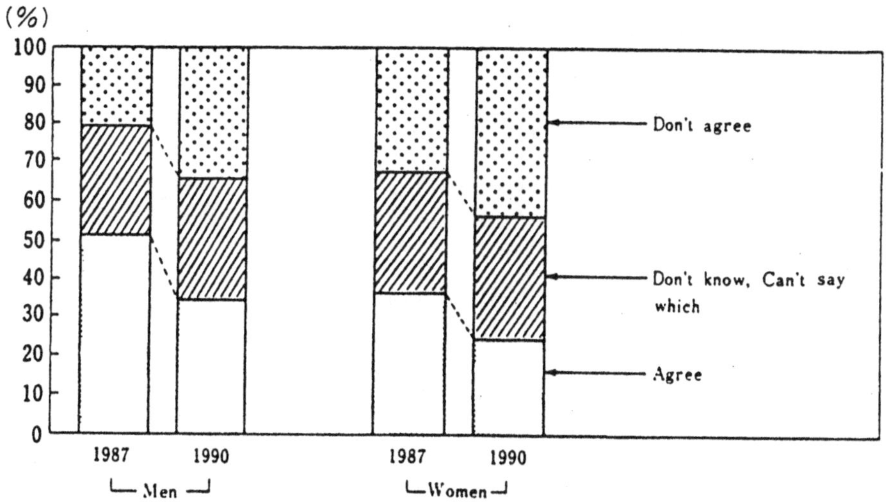

Figure 43. Changes in views and opinions on traditional belief: "men should hold jobs and women should stay home and do home work."

Source: Office of the Prime Minister, *Poll on Women* (1990)
Note: Replies to the question "Do you agree or not agree on the traditional belief that 'Men should hold jobs and women should stay home and do housework'?"

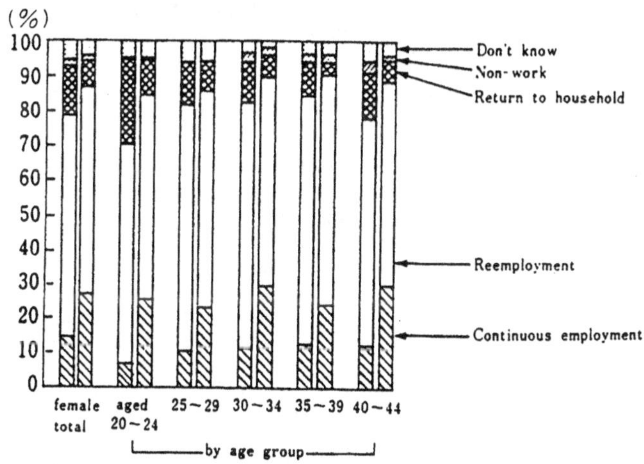

Figure 44. Desirable employment pattern for female workers.

Source: Office of the Prime Minister, *Poll on Women's Employment* (1989)
Note: Left column: Replies to the question "Which employment pattern do you generally consider most desirable throughout women's lives?"
Right column: Replies to the question "How should women work in all stages of their life provided that systematized maternity and childcare leave and complete childcare facilities are offered."
Choices for the survey were:
"Continuous employment" (continue to work long)
"Reemployment" (quit work upon marriage and childbirth but resume work after short breaks)
"Return to household" (quit work upon marriage and childbirth to be a housewife)
"Non-work" (do not work)
"Don't know" (do not know and others)

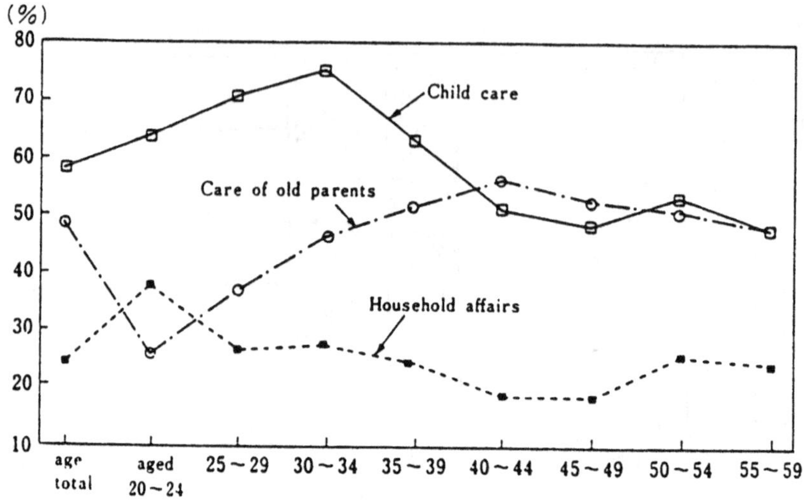

Figure 45. Reasons why women find trouble continuing work.

Source: Office of the Prime Minister, *Poll on Female Employment* (1989)
Note: The question asked in the poll is "What hampers or presents do you think as an obstacle of women's continuous employment?" "Care of oldparents" also means care of sick family members.

their employment. By age group, women, particularly those aged between 30 and 34, list childcare as constituting a barrier, while those aged 40 and over cite care of old parents as presenting an obstacle to their continued employment (Fig. 45).

The Effects of Female Workers' Lives on Their Employment

Childcare hampers female employment. Of the married women between the ages of 20-to-24 and 40-to-49, approximately 70 percent of those who have no infants and those who have pre-schoolers have jobs. The percentage is slightly below that of unmarried women in the same age group (80%). Of the unmarried working women, over 90 percent devoted the significant portion of their time to work. On the other hand, many married working women work while doing household chores. About half of those in the age group of 30–39 and over who have no young children and of those in all age groups who have pre-schoolers combine jobs with housework. Furthermore, only 20–40 percent of married women, whose children do not attend pre-schools, have jobs – of which more than 50 percent work while doing domestic duties (Fig. 46).

Let us look at employment of married women in the 25–34 age group in terms of the youngest child's age and the household makeup; 28.7 percent women of "households composed of a couple with children" are in the labour force when the youngest child is a pre-schooler. The figure is far below the 55.6 percent of those from such households when the youngest child attends a primary school. On the other hand, 52.3 percent of women from "households composed of a couple with children and parents (or so-called three-generation families)" are in the labour force when the youngest child is a pre-schooler and 66.7 percent work when the youngest child is a primary school student. The ratio of short-time employees to women of "households of a couple with children" is high. As we have seen, many women of nuclear families stay home and raise children and many working women of such families find it difficult to work full time (Table 47).

Looking at the time spent working daily, unmarried working women spend over six hours, but married counterparts with a pre-schooler allocate more than five hours and those whose children do not attend pre-schools around 4.5 hours. This reveals that women who must spend some time on childcare and domestic chores are compelled to work shorter hours than those who do not have to (Fig. 48).

Care of old parents also seems to hamper female employment. A shade over 50 percent of women who don't have to care for old parents at home have jobs, while slightly less than 40 percent of those who have to care have jobs.

Table 47. Effects of children and parents on employment of married women (aged 25–34)

	Household couple only	Household of couple with their parent(s)	Household of couple with their child(ren)					Household of couple with their child(ren) and parent(s)				
			Total	With the youngest child attending day nursery or kindergarten (0–6 years old)	With the youngest child attending elementary school (7–12 years old)	With the youngest child attending junior high school (13–14 years old)	With the youngest child aged 15-and-over	Total	With the youngest child attending day nursery or kindergarten (0–6 years old)	With the youngest child attending elementary school (7–12 years old)	With the youngest child attending junior high school (13–14 years old)	With the youngest child aged 15-and-over
Labour force (10000)	47	10	99	78	20	1	–	53	45	8	–	–
Labour force participation rate (%)	55.3	71.4	32.0	28.7	55.6	–	–	54.1	52.3	66.7	–	–
No. of employees (10000)	40	8	70	54	15	1	–	39	32	7	–	–
(Note) of employees working less than 35 hours	15	2	34	26	7	–	–	12	9	1	–	–
Rate of employees working less than 35 hours to all employees	37.5	25.0	48.6	48.1	46.7	–	–	30.8	28.1	14.3	–	–

Source: Statistics Bureau, Management and Coordination Agency, *Special Survey of the Labour Force Survey* (1990).
Note: Represents hours worked weekly.

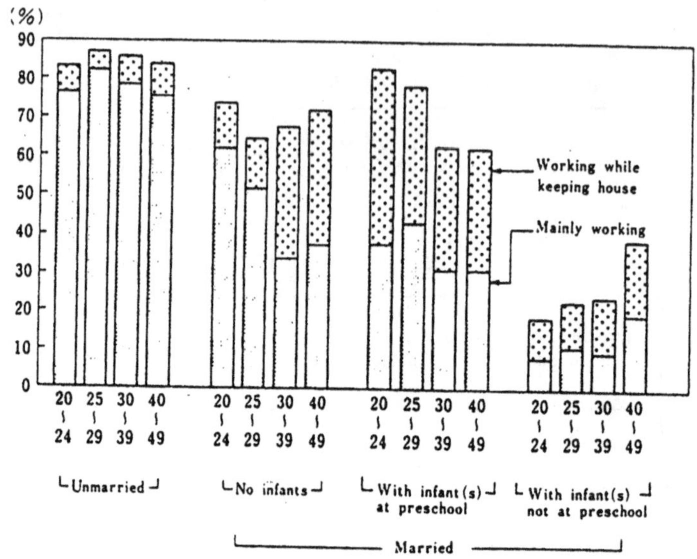

Figure 46. Rate of working women by marital status, by age group.

Source: Statistics Bureau, Management and Coordination Agency, *The Survey on Time Use and Leisure Activities* (1986) (Special Tabulation)
Note: "Infants" mean children under six.

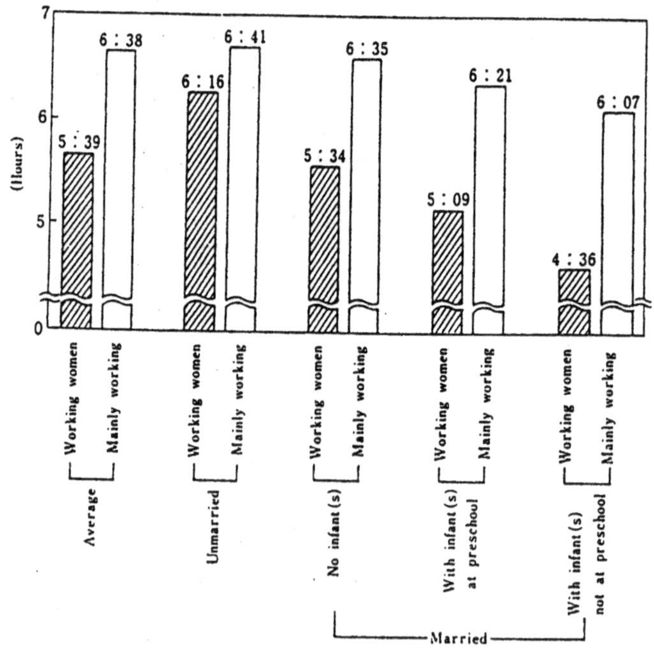

Figure 48. Working hours for working women.

Source: Statistics Bureau, Management and Coordination Agency, *The Survey on Time Use and Leisure Activities* (1986) (Special Tabulation)
Note: 1) Daily average of overall weekly hours worked
2) Same as Fig. 46

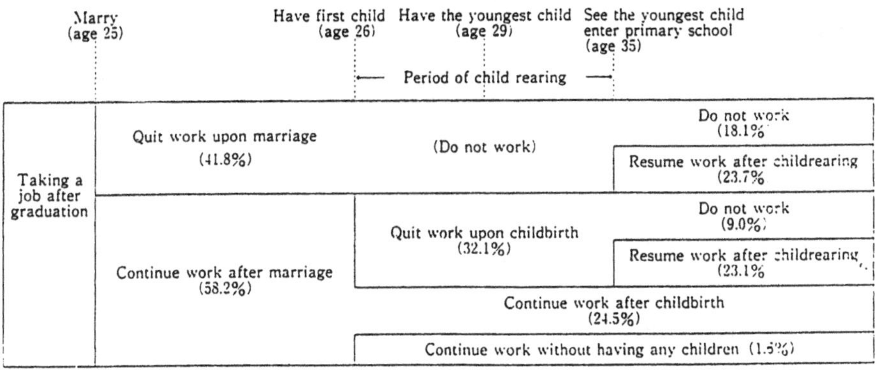

Figure 49. Relations of marriage, childbirth and childcare to work seen from women's attitudes.

Source: Institution of Population Problems, Ministry of Health and Welfare, *9th Japanese National Fertility Survey* (1987)
Notes:
1) Based upon replies to the question for wives under 50 "What shape would your life take when you look back on the past?"
2) The median value was taken for each of ages at which the women marriages, at which she has the first child and at which she has the youngest child (the second and the third child). (The proportion of first to third birth in the total was 97.0% in 1989)

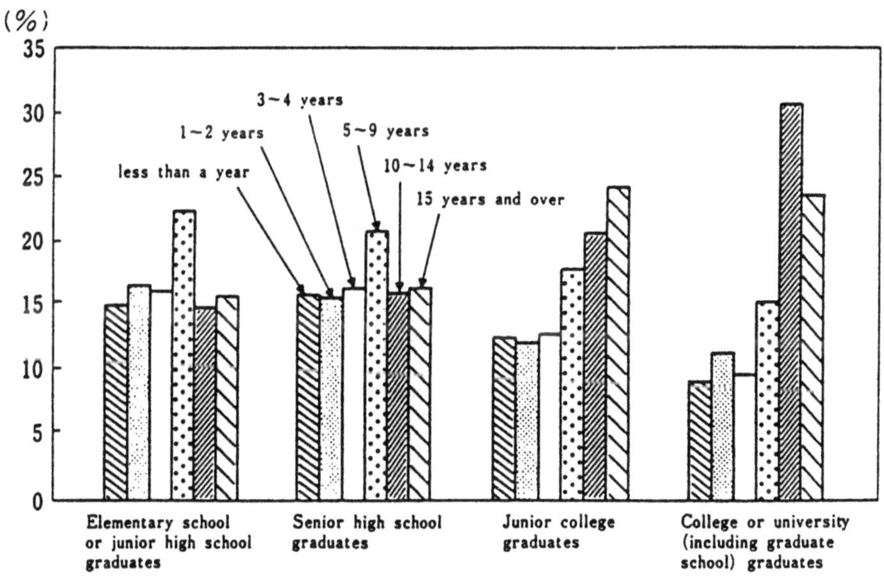

Figure 50. Years of continuous employment of women aged 35–39 by education.

Source: Statistics Bureau, Management and Coordination Agency, *Employment Status Survey*

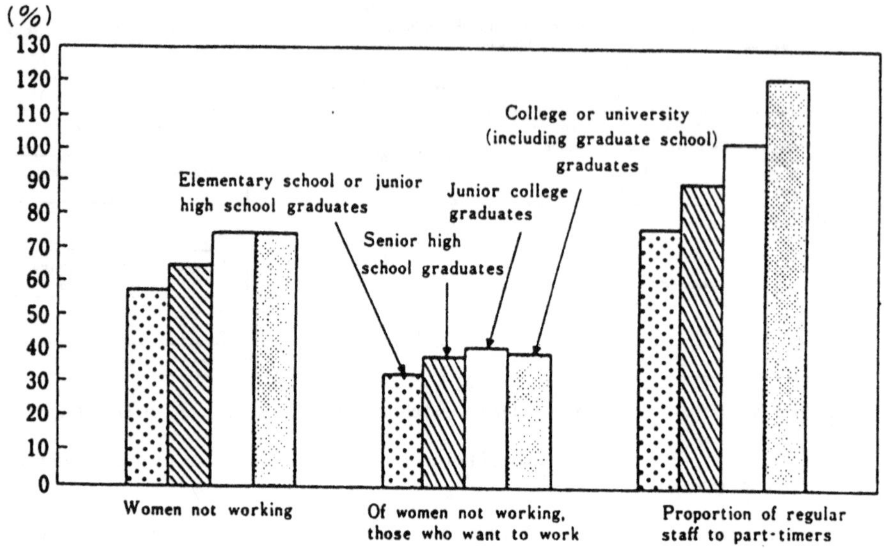

Figure 51. Employment status of women who once quit-work because of marriage and childrearing by education.

Source: Statistic Bureau, Management and Coordination Agency, *Employment Status Survey* (1987) (Special Tabulation)
Note: "Women not working" and "Of women not working, those who want to work" represent the proportion to total women who once quit "because of marriage and childrearing" for each education.

Female Workers' Jobs and Lifestyles

Let us look at an average women's life pattern based upon a survey of married women under 50. Responding to a question "What shape would your ultimate life take when you look back on the past," 41.8 percent of respondents would quit (left) work upon marriage, while 32.1 percent would do (did) so upon childbirth, thus bringing the retiree total to nearly three-quarters of the surveyed. However, almost half, or 46.8 percent, said that they would return (returned) to their jobs after bringing up their children. This in effect means about three-fourths will find (found) employment after marriage, manifesting women's strong desire to work (Fig. 49).

Take those in the 35-to-39 age group, for instance – most of whom finished schooling over 10 years ago, 45.2 percent of junior college leavers and technical college leavers have continued to work for over 10 years, 10 percent point more than elementary school leavers and junior high school leavers (36.3%), while 54.6 percent of college and university graduates have done so, 20 percent point more (31.9). The statistics thus show the tendency for women with higher education to work longer (Fig. 50).

Observing the proportion of women not working by educational attainment to those who quit work because of marriage and childcare, 74.8 percent of junior and technical college leavers and 75.1 percent of college and university graduates, nearly 20 percent point more than the proportion of primary and junior high school leavers (56.5%), respectively. This suggests that while those with higher educational attainment tend to work in the longer term, they would rather stay home once they stop working upon marriage and childbirth (Fig. 51).

Section 4 Employment Management of Female Workers

The proportion of establishments which have adopted childcare leave is rising. In 1989, 19.2 percent of the establishments surveyed introduced the system and 23.5 percent of all female workers benefited from it. The system is adopted notably in services (42.1%) and at the establishments with 500 employees and over (25.3%) (Table 52). Incidentally, the Law Concerning Child Care Leave was enacted in May 1991 and will go into effect in April, 1992.

Table 52. Proportion of establishments with childcare leave system by industry, size (unit: %)

Industry – size	1972	1973	1975	1977	1979	1982	1986	1989
Total	2.3	4.3	5.7	6.3	6.6	14.3	14.6	19.2 (23.5)
Manufacturing	1.1	4.1	7.1	4.6	5.2	5.2	4.4	9.5
Electricity, gas, heat supply and water	–	–	–	–	–	11.2	22.7	
Transport and communication	9.4	9.8	9.4	12.4	11.6	12.1	11.2	16.3
Wholesale, retail trade, eating and drinking places	1.0	2.2	3.6	3.1	4.6	7.6	10.2	
Financing and insurance	0.6	3.2	2.2	2.8	2.9	3.4	4.4	16.2
Service	1.9	4.5	4.5	12.6	13.8	42.9	40.0	42.1
500 and more employees	7.1	11.4	15.0	17.8	17.8	19.9	20.1	25.3
100–499 employees	4.6	6.6	8.8	12.3	13.2	13.8	13.9	18.0
30–99 employees	1.2	3.2	4.4	4.0	4.0	14.3	14.7	19.4

Source: Ministry of Labour, *Survey on Implementation of Female Protection* (1971–1985), *Survey on Women Workers Employment Management* (1988).
Notes:
1) Principal industries alone are shown for comparison by industry. Figures for "total", however, cover all industries.
2) The category "service" includes education for a survey conducted in and after 1982.
3) A survey on childcare leave was conducted as of June 1, 1972 for a 1972 survey, as of December 31, 1973 for a 1973 survey, as of June 1, 1975 for a 1974 survey and as February 1 of the following year for surveys of 1976 and beyond.
4) The parenthesized figures in the column of total for 1989 denote the proportion of women workers to whom childcare leave system is applicable.

The percentage of those establishments which implement a home-care leave system rose from 8.7 percent in 1982 to 13.6 percent in 1989; however, the proportion is smaller than that of those establishments which adopt childcare leave. Asked about who did most of the care of old parents at home, the highest, or 51.5 percent of male respondents said the wife did, while the largest, or 43.5 percent of female respondents said they did it themselves. The figures thus show care of old parents give more of the responsibilities to women.

The percentage of those establishments which have introduced a reemployment system for women jumped from 5.6 percent in 1986 to 16.6 percent in 1989.

Only 2.9 percent of all enterprises have launched career tracking in personnel management by course. The introduction of this system, however, is notable in part of the industries, such as finance and insurance (21.2%) and of the enterprises, such as the one with 5,000 workers and over (42.3%) (Table 53).

Table 53. State of enterprises' introduction of career tracking in personnel management (unit: %)

Industry – size	Total	Already introduced	Not yet introduced	Plan for introduction: Plan to introduce	Do not plan to introduce	No replies
Total	100.0	2.9	97.1	4.7		
			(100.0)	(4.8)	(95.0)	(0.1)
Mining	100.0	5.3	94.7	2.9		
			(100.0)	(3.1)	(96.9)	(–)
Construction	100.0	2.0	98.0	6.6		
			(100.0)	(6.7)	(93.3)	(0.0)
Manufacturing	100.0	2.3	97.6	3.9		
			(100.0)	(4.0)	(95.8)	(0.2)
Electricity, gas, heat supply and water	100.0	2.9	97.1	1.6		
			(100.0)	(1.8)	(98.2)	(–)
Transport and communication	100.0	1.5	98.5	1.9		
			(100.0)	(6.4)	(97.8)	(0.3)
Wholesale, retail trade, eating and drinking places	100.0	5.2	94.8	6.4		
			(100.0)	(6.7)	(93.2)	(0.0)
Financing and insurance	100.0	21.2	78.8	9.9		
			(100.0)	(12.7)	(86.8)	(0.6)
Real estate	100.0	6.7	93.3	3.3		
			(100.0)	(3.6)	(96.4)	(–)
Service	100.0	1.5	98.5	4.7		
			(100.0)	(4.8)	(95.2)	(–)
5000 or more employees	100.0	42.3	57.7	11.3		
			(100.0)	(19.4)	(76.7)	(3.9)
1000–4999 employees	100.0	25.3	74.5	11.1		
			(100.0)	(14.9)	(84.4)	(0.7)
300–999 employees	100.0	11.4	88.6	9.6		
			(100.0)	(10.8)	(89.1)	(0.1)
100–299 employees	100.0	4.3	95.7	4.3		
			(100.0)	(4.4)	(95.3)	(0.2)
30–99 employees	100.0	0.9	99.0	4.2		
			(100.0)	(4.3)	(95.7)	(0.1)

Source: Ministry of Labour, *Survey on Women Workers Employment Management* (1989).
Note: Figures in parenthesis denote percentages for each item with "Have not introduced" as 100.

APPENDIX 2

FOR PROMOTION OF WELFARE OF PART-TIME WORKERS

- Part-time workers are increasing in number every year. As of 1992, the number was 8,680,000 (among which 5,920,000 were female).
- Two-thirds of part-time workers are housewives.
- 85.0% of female part-time workers are distributed among the following three industries; 1) the wholesale, retail and restaurant industry; 2) the service industry; 3) and the manufacturing industry.
- Part-time workers are also participating in technical-professional occupations.
- The amount of the hourly basic wage paid to female part-time workers is \809 on the average.
- 40% of female part-time workers work 'to help family finances.'
- A majority of female part-time workers choose to work part time because part-time work allows time schedule flexibility.
- 83% of female part-time workers hope to continue working part-time.
- 30% of female part-time workers adjust their working hours so that their annual income may not go

beyond the threshold of \1,000,000.

- 98% of establishments clarify working conditions, however, only 30% of those reduce it to writing.
- The percentage of employers which provide vocational training for female part-time workers is low.
- 60% of establishments conduct medical examinations for part-time workers.
- The proportion of establishments whose welfare schemes cover part-time workers is low.

1. Part-Time Workers Are Increasing in Number Every Year. the Percentage of Part-Time Employees among all Female Employees Has Grown 10.2% for these Ten Years.

The number of part-time workers has been increasing since about 1960 with housewives as the main source of this increase. In particular, from 1965 to 75, and since 1985, the percentage has grown remarkably. The number of part-time employees (except those in the agriculutural and forestry industries), who work less than 35 hours a week, has grown from 1,330,000 (among which 570,000 are female) in 1960 to 8,680,000 (5,920,000 are female) as of 1992. The percentage of part-time employees among all employees reached 17.3% (30.7% among female employees) in 1992. Especially it has been increasing remarkably among female employees, which has grown by 10.2% for these ten years.

2. Part-Time Workers Are Changing Greatly in Quality

(1) Diversification of reasons to take part-time work (from housewives to help family finances, to housewives who hope to engage in professional jobs, the aged, students etc.)
The percentages of housewives (female part-time workers with husbands), those aged of fifty-five and over, and students, among part-time workers, are about 65%, 16%, and 12% respectively.

(2) The length of employment is 4.8 years on average.
Formerly, part-time workers were seen as workers who were supplementary, temporary, and easy to change their places of employment, however, the proportion of part-time workers who work as basic and constant work forces has been growing recently. Accordingly, the length of service of part-time workers on average has greatly increased from 2.9 years in 1976 to 4.8 years in 1992.

(3) 85.0% of female part-time workers are distributed in the wholesale, retail and restaurant industry, the service industry, or the manufacturing industry.
Main industries in which female part-time employees work are: the wholesale, retail and restaurant industry (2,050,000 people; 34.6%); the service industry (1,720,000 people; 29.1%); and the manufacturing industry (1,260,000 people; 21.6%). To sum up, 85.0% of female part-time workers are employed in these three industries.
In analyzing the changes in these last ten years, the proportion of part-time workers in the wholesale, retail and restaurant industry and the service industry among those in all industries has increased to some degree. The percentage of part-time workers in the manufacturing industry among those in all industries has decreased in spite of a increase of absolute number of female part-time employees in this industry. We can figure that the number of female part-time employees has grown especially in the tertiary industries.
A search for the proportion of female part-time employees among all female employees in each industry, shows the highest proportion to be 38.7% in the wholesale, retail and restaurant industry, and, in the following order, 31.0% in the transport and communication industry, 30.0% in the construction industry, 28.4% in the service industry, and 27.3% in the banking, insurance and real-estate industry. The ones in the manufacturing industry and the other industries are 24 to 26%.
In all industries the proportion of part-time workers tends to increase year by year.

(4) Part-time workers are also participating in technical- professional occupations.
5.0% of part-time employees engaged in technical-professional occupations which were once seen for such workers to be difficult to access. The main occupations in which part-time employees engage are sales and commerce (27.3%), and service (19.1%), etc.
To research a percentage of part-time workers among all workers in each occupation, the three highest ones are 61.6% in transport and manual labor, 53.9% in sale and commerce, and 49.2% in service. Even in technical-professional occupations it is 13.3%, which tells us part-time work is an important form of work in such occupations.

3. Actual Working Conditions of Part-Time Workers

(1) Employers Are Required to Manage Working Time of Part-Time Workers Appropriately

1. Normal working hours a day of female part-time workers on an average are 5.8 hours, and working days a month are 20.9 days in June 1992. To survey the changes, those tend to decrease partly affected by reduction of working hours of regular workers based on execution of the working-hours reduction policy.
2. To figure the working hours in one day of part-time workers, the starting time and the finishing time are broadly distributed because of the diversification of needs of the employer and the required flexibility on the part of the employee.

   The starting time is most frequently between 9:00~10:00 (45.6%), and the finishing time is between 16:00~17:00 (30.0%).
3. The Labor Standards Act regulates that part-time workers who meet certain requirements receive paid annual leave calculated proportionately, which is to increase gradually with the length of service to the upper limit of 14 days. However, we see many cases in which part-time workers do not receive paid annual leave though they meet the requirements.

   The percentage of female part-time workers who receive paid annual leave among those who worked 80% and over of the working days in the previous year, is 54.4%, and the average days in those are 10.9 days.
4. Most female part-time workers choose to work part time because of their wish to combine their occupation with family responsibilities. It is very important for many of them that working hours are short and do not prevent them from spending time with their families, etc.. However, more than 20% of them work overtime in practice.

The percentage of female part-time workers who worked overtime among those who worked in September 1990, is 20.8%, and the average overtime hours per month was 8.0 hours.

(2) The amount of an hourly basic wage paid to female part-time workers is \809 on an average

1. Wages paid to female part-time workers, are the most frequently paid as an hourly wage (84.4%), and, in order, a daily wage (7.2%), a monthly wage (6.2%), and a wage on a percentage basis (1.4%).
2. A The amount of an hourly basic wage of female part-time workers was \809 on average in June 1992, which had increased by \39 from 1991 to 92. The amount of annual bonus and the other special allowances was \98,800, which had increased by \6,400 (6.9%) from 1991 to 92.
3. The majority (70.6%) of establishments decide how much they will pay their newly employed female part-time workers with reference to 'a market price of part-time workers with the same occupation in the region.'
4. To see what allowances are given to female part-time workers, 63.7% of establishments give a commuting allowance. 40.4% increase wages of female part-time workers regularly, 35.1% raise their basic wage rate. 60.5%, which is relatively high, of establishments give them bonuses.

Only 12.2% of establishments have retirement allowance schemes which apply to part-time workers.

4. Part-Time Workers' Thoughts on Working

(1) The proportion of female part-time workers whose reason to work is 'to help family finances' is 40%.

The reasons why female part-time workers start to work: The highest percentage (43.7%) of female part-time workers work because they 'help family finances', and in order, 'improve a level of life' (15.6%), 'to make a main income for life' (14.9%), 'to make the most of leisure time' (14.2%), and 'the other reasons' (11.6%).

(2) A majority of female part-time workers choose to work part time on account of flexibility of time.

In analyzing the reasons why they choose to work part time, we can see clearly that from their attitude toward flexibility of time, 64.8% of female part-time workers choose to work part time because they 'hope to work when they like,' 34.3% 'hope to shorten working hours and working days,' and 24.1% 'for household and childcare.'

(3) Female part-time workers are relatively highly satisfied with their working time and the content of work.

In analyzing how content they are with their working conditions etc., it seems that they are content with their 'working time' (63.1%) and the 'contents of work' (56.4%) to a relatively high degree. On the other hand, there is a low satisfaction with 'welfare schemes and facilities in the establishment' (21.7%), their 'rise in wage and promotion' (19.5%), and their 'vocational training' (15.0%).

(4) More than 80% of female part-time workers hope to continue working part time.
To analyze what form of working they hope to work in, 83.2% of female part-time workers 'hope to continue working in the present form,' partly because they did choose part-time work voluntarily. Only 11.0% of female part-time workers 'hope to change the present form.'

(5) 60% of female part-time workers wish to engage in a job which is worth doing and interests them.
To see what jobs female part-time workers hope to do in the future, the highest percentage (60.2%) of them hope to engage in 'a job which is worth doing and interests them.' Next, we can see many female part-time workers who wish to do a job which is a light burden to them, such as 'a job physically easy to do' (15.2%) and 'a simple and supplementary job' (11.8%). However, 4.0% of female part-time workers hope to engage in 'a main responsible job.'

(6) 30% of female part-time workers adjust their working hours.
Some part-time workers adjust their working hours so that their income may not go beyond a certain threshold. Because they are obliged to pay taxes and social assurance contributions, and the spouse allowance paid to their husbands by their husbands' employers may be cut off, when the income of part-time workers exceeds a certain threshold.
To begin with, there are 27.3% of female part-time workers whose 'annual income has no possibility to be over \1,000,000.' Nevertheless, 30.4% of female part-time workers 'adjust their working hours' when their annual income may go beyond \1,000,000. The proportion of female part-time workers who 'do not adjust their working hours though thier annual income may go over \1,000,000,' is 23.0%.
In addition, an average annual income of female part-time workers was \959,000, and 62.9% of those earned less than \1,000,000, in 1989.

5. Personnel Management of Part-Time Workers

(1) Employers take measures mainly on wages to recruit good part-time workers and make them stay in the enterprise.

The proportion of employers who plan to hire good part-time workers is growing. These employers wish to make part-time workers become basic work forces by vocational training and correct personnel evaluation, and to make them stay in the enterprise.

1. In reference to measures to recruit good part-time workers, the highest percentage (36.8%) of employers 'pay appropriate wages to their job and ability,' and in order, 'make their hourly wages higher than a market price' (19.9%), 'raise their wages regularly' (22.6%). We figure that employers take measures mainly on wages to hire good part-time workers.
2. As measures to make part-time workers stay in the enterprise, a high percentage of employers 'pay appropriate wages to their jobs and ability' (40.1%), and ' raise their wages regularly' (22.6%). Employers who take (one or all of) these two measures amount to 60%.

(2) Only 30% of establishments clarify working conditions of part-time workers in writing.
Concerning working conditions, there are various differences not only between those of part-time workers and those of regular workers, but also among part-time workers. So, it is desirable to clarify in writing the working conditions of part-time workers. However, there are not so many employers who hand out a notice of employment or work rules etc., when they hire part-time workers.

1. 98.1% of establishments clarify working conditions when hiring. However, 66.5% of those 'mainly explain by word of mouth.' 15.8% of those 'mainly hand a document such as a notice of employment,' and 13.9% 'mainly hand work rules and conclude a employment contract in writing.' Accordingly, only 29.7% of establishments clarify working conditions in writing in any form.
2. About 40% (precisely 38.8%) of establishments 'have no work rules which apply to part-time employees.' It is required for such establishments 'to apply special work rules for part-time workers to them' (20.5% in practice), 'to make addition of special regulations for part-time workers to work rules for regular workers and apply them' (7.6% in practice), or 'to apply work rules for regular workers to part-time workers correspondingly' (33.1% in practice), etc.

Even in the establishments which have work rules for part-time workers, only 30% of those consult the opinions of part-time workers when they modify the rules. 70.0% of those 'do not consult the opinions of part-time workers.'

(3) 30% of part-time workers are hired on fixed-term contracts.
In general, people see that most part-time workers are hired on fixed-term contracts. But, to research the periods of contracts of part-time workers, 60% of those are hired on contracts without fixed-term. The proportion of part-time workers who are hired through fixed-term contracts is 31.1%.
On the other hand, to see how many establishments give a notice of expiration, only half of establishments, among those which hire part-time workers on fixed-term contracts (30.4% of all), 'give a thirty-day's notice of expiration (which is regulated by the Governmental Guidelines on Part-time Work).'

(4) The proportion of employers which give vocational training to female part-time workers is low.
Because most employers see female part-time workers as simple and supplementary work forces, not so many employers intend to make effective use of abilities of part-time workers yet.
In analyzing how employers carry out vocational training for part-time workers, we see that the highest percentage (37.7%) of employers do not give training because 'vocational training is not necessary for the jobs which female part-time workers engage in.' On the other hand, 21.3% of employers 'carry out vocational training when and after hiring,' 6.3% 'carry out only after hiring,' and 15.4% 'train through OJT (On the Job Training).'

(5) The rate of affiliation of part-time workers with the Unemployment Insurance, the Health Insurance, and the Welfare Pension Insurance, is respectively less than 30% .
Less than 30% of part-time workers are affiliated with the Unemployment Insurance (29.0%), the Health Insurance/the Welfare Pension Insurance (24.8%), respectively.

(6) 60% of establishments give medical examinations for part-time workers.
60.5% of establishments give periodical medical examinations for part-time workers.

(7) The percentage of establishments whose welfare schemes cover part-time workers is low.
Employers establish various welfare schemes and facilities for regular workers to promote their welfare. However, employers often make differences between regular workers and part-time workers on application of the schemes and use of the facilities. 7.8% of establishments apply the property build-up scheme to part-time workers, 3.3% apply the company pension scheme, 25.9% allow to use welfare facilities.

(8) Hence, it is desirable to make appropriate use of part-time workers to their character.
Part-time working is a form of work which both employers and employees need. And in consideration of a tendency of need for work force in future, part-time working is to be a more important form of work. So, it is required that we make the best use of part-time working from now on.
Therefore, positive use of part-time workers, such as extention of the range of occupation in which part-time workers engage, and advancement of some part-time workers to a regular worker's position, are desirable.
However, in the present situation, part-time workers are not necessarily most appropriately matched to their skills.

1. In an analysis of how employers make the best use of female part-time workers (M.A.), we see the highest percentage (42.5%) of employers 'carry out vocational training and make the best use of them,' and in order, 37.1% of employers 'make effective use of them in suitable jobs for women,' and 35.2% 'hire skilled and/or qualified persons and make full use of them immediately.' The percentage of employers who 'make use of female part-time workers without making a difference between male workers and female workers' is 18.7%.
2. In an analysis of what schemes establishments introduce to make effective use of part-time workers or not, only 10.7% of establishments carry out 'advancement to a regular worker's position,' which is the most frequent scheme. 3.3% of establishments introduce 'a qualification system based on job evaluation,' and 1.7% carry out 'promotion to an administrative position,' those percentages are much less.

APPENDIX 3

JAPAN INSTITUTE OF LABOUR, JAPANESE WORKING LIFE PROFILE (1994)

(67) Number of Female Part-Time Workers and Their Ratio to the Total Number of Female Employees

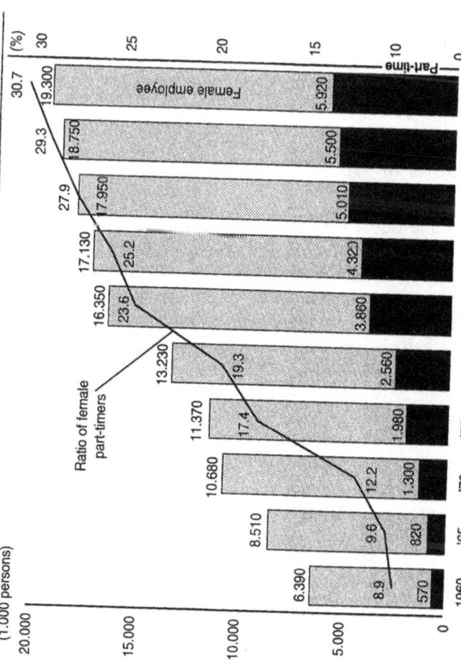

Source Management and Coordination Agency, *Labor Force Survey*.
Note Female part-time workers are those whose working hours during the week surveyed are less than 35 hours.

(68) Structure of Female Part-Time Workers

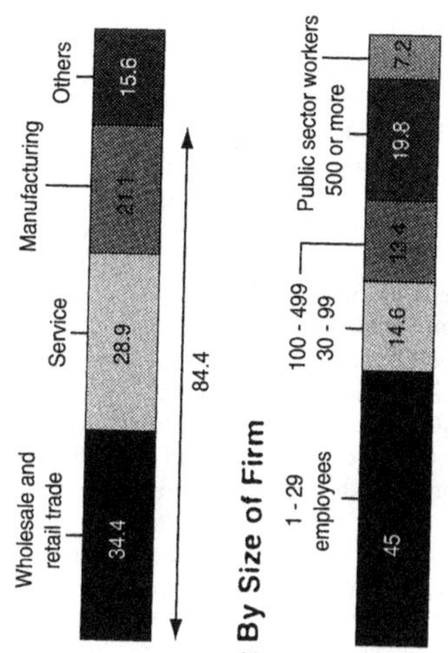

Source: Management and Coordination Agency, *Labor Force Survey*.
Notes: 1) Total number of female part-time workers was 5,960,000 in 1991.
2) "Others" include agriculture, finance and insurance; real estate, construction, transport and communication, electricity, gas, water and heat supply; and Government.

APPENDIX 4

WHITE PAPER ON LABOUR 1994 (P.252~P.258)

2) The Present State of The Management and Assistance of Continued Employment for Female Workers Employment

Attitudes Towards Working Patterns and Increase of Continued Employment

According to the 'Poll of The Will to Work' (1992) mentioned above, attitudes about what constitutes a desirable pattern for the female workers are as follows.

68 percent of female workers in the 20-to-64 age group, said 'despite of quitting work upon marriage, childbirth etc., temporarily, desire to return to their jobs after break' (call·'The Model of Re-Employment'), 15.4 percent of those said 'desire to work as long as possible'. It seems that the attitude of women is for re-employment. However, they said that the following factors are important, so that they may display their ability as professionals: 1) childcare leave system (50.5%) : 2) nursing leave system (26.1%) : 3) reasonable treatment in company (42.5%) : 4) equal opportunities of sexes (21:8%) : 5) a revolution of social consciousness (25.4%), etc. (Table 52). According to the 'Poll on Female Employment' (Office of The Prime Minister, 1989) many female workers cite 'childcare' (58.6%) and 'care of an elder and a patient' (48.7%) and 'insufficient working conditions and system' (28.0%) as reasons for making it difficult for them to continue their work. As we could seen above, a number of women prefer 'The Model of Re-Employment' not only by their desire, but also by reason of the environment surrounding them.

According to the 'Basic Survey on Wage Structure' mentioned above, the ratio of female workers is as follows. Namely, those in their late 20s and early 30s have decreased rapidly. Only 10 percent of them work despite marriage, childbirth, and childcare. Comparing 1992 with 1987, the rate of continued female workers of the same generation, however, has increased and the increase is remarkable, particularly in university graduates (Fig. 3-(3)-5).

Although the ratio of continued female workers increases constantly, the level is still lower when compared with that of males. This result shows that child related events care problem and nursing problem and discriminatory treatment between the sexes constitute a barrier to their continued employment. From this perspective, first, this paper studies the problem regarding the present state and the problems of managing female workers. Second, this paper will concentrate on problems for harmonizing working life with family life. It will attempt to study problems regarding childcare and nursing problems. Below is an outline of the analysis.

Present State and Problem of Management Female Workers

Five years have passed since the Equal Employment Opportunity Law (EEOL) went into effect. After the enforcement of the EEOL, some aspects of employment they have been improved a employees. Enterprises not only observe the law, but also wish to use more female ability. For instance, before EEOL went into effect, enterprises in general recruited male and female separately; but after the enforcement of the law, enterprises recruiting both male and female have greatly increased. Now, more females follow careers in the fields of business and clerical. Meanwhile, according to the 'Basic Survey on Female Workers Employment Management' (1992), 34 percent of enterprises recruited only new male university graduates, 47.5 percent only new male university graduates from science and engineering, and 5.3 percent put women in auxiliary positions. Thus ,it is expected that further improvements will be made.

After the enforcement of the EEOL, 3.8 percent of all enterprises (it is more notable in large enterprises) introduced so-called 'Employment Management by Course'. Unsuitable treatment of women, however, can still be found in enterprises adopting the system. It is hoped that enterprises should operate employment management in accordance with the EEOL and 'The Desirable Employment Management by Course'. In addition, it is necessary for female workers to improve working environment conditions that are in the way of developing and utilizing female abilities (e.g., fixed consciousness of the roles played by both sexes), and they should not only promote a vocational sense, but also actively utilize that improved condition themselves.

Assistance for Harmonizing Working Life and Family Life

Since the Child Care Leaves Law (CCLL) went into effect in April 1992, the number of enterprises which adopted the child care leave system, particularly in large enterprises, have increased rapidly in 1990–1993 (Fig. 3-(3)-6). Establishment of this system, however, is delayed in enterprises that enforcement of the law be stayed for the time being (employing 30 or less employees). Thinking that the law will be enforced against all enterprises from April 1995, it is important for labor welfare that these enterprises improve their 'Work–Rules' within 1994.

Furthermore, it is necessary that other factors should be improved, so that the system may be effective. The first is a problem of economics due to the leave period. According to the 'Basic Survey on Female Workers Employment Management' mentioned above, 39.3 percent of the enterprises pay women themselves or from resources allocated from a cooperative society. 60.6 percent of enterprises pay by adopting 'a monthly allowance', which is composed mainly of a 'considerable sum of social insurance of employee town expense' (76.3%).

The second problem is how to maintain and promote vocational abilities, so that female workers may smoothly return to their job. According to the 'Basic Survey on Female Workers Employment Management' (1993) mentioned above, 37.7 percent of the enterprises take measures for maintaining and promoting vocational abilities of female workers on childcare leave. The measures are 'furnishing information on female workers during the leave period' (85.1%) and 'educational campaigns for returning to their job' etc. The measures are extremely important for female workers in order to smoothly return to their jobs. Government, therefore, is about to introduce the system through supporting as 'promotion subsidy', to enable female workers to return their jobs. However, it is necessary to devise a measure to assess the situation of each worker. Since, the period of child care is long, and a way of returning are different according to the occupation of individual workers, as well as to occupational status and to vocational sense, etc.

The third problem is how to improve the environment after running out of child care leave. A great number of enterprises (91.3%) decide that leave should end when 'the child becomes the age of one year'. According to the 'Poll on Female Employment' (1989) mentioned above, many women are raising babies and children and therefore require that employers should adopt child care leaves and release women from work for childcare and provide childcare facilities, so that women could continue their jobs (Table 53). In view of this, it is important to improve the environment and to release women from work for childcare and to provide childcare facilities, after child care leaves run out.

In addition, the government decided to establish a child care leave benefit systems employment insurance, so that female workers may easily take childcare leave and smoothly return to their jobs. At present, the 'The Bill on Partial revision of Employment Insurance Law, etc.' including the benefit system is under consideration at the 129th session of the National Assembly.

In the past, nursing problem was also regarded as a private problem, with the emphasis on the women's problem. With the emergence of an aging society, however, the nursing problem has became an important problem for all of society. Therefore, there should be an endeavor to substantially improve nursing services and nursing facilities, under the ten-year economic development plan for promoting health and welfare of the aged (Gold Plan).

The fact is that family trends are now toward nuclear families, and being a people cannot always give primary care. Society takes it for granted that male and female work together, and they have to leave for childcare reasons. Family care is, therefore, a very important problem to the employee who desires to continue employment. In fact, there are many employees who quit their jobs or change their employment or working conditions to fulfil care needs. Many say they 'cannot continue work' if they have families wanting care (Table 54). Most employee's depend on the enterprises in the welfare system (in case of nursing) which is the nursing leave system and, secondly, the system to choose working time for care (Table 55).

It is hoped, therefore, that government and the employer not only improve nursing facilities and nursing services, but also extend the nursing leave system, so that employees who have families wanting care may both provide care and work. According to the 'Basic Survey on Female Workers Employment Management' (1993) mentioned above, 16.3 percent of enterprises have a nursing leave system. This is, however, still insufficient though the extension rate of the system is over the majority (51.9%) of enterprises which employ more than 500 workers (Fig. 3-(3)-6). The Ministry of Labor, therefore, has attempted to facilitate the nursing leave system on the grounds of the 'Guideline on The Nursing Leave System, etc.' To promote the nursing leave system, it is necessary to enact such a system. There are, however, various factors, for instance, families wanting care and workers who care for families, etc. It is necessary to study these factors sufficiently before any enactment. The above problems, Therefore, are now under study from the special and technical viewpoints.

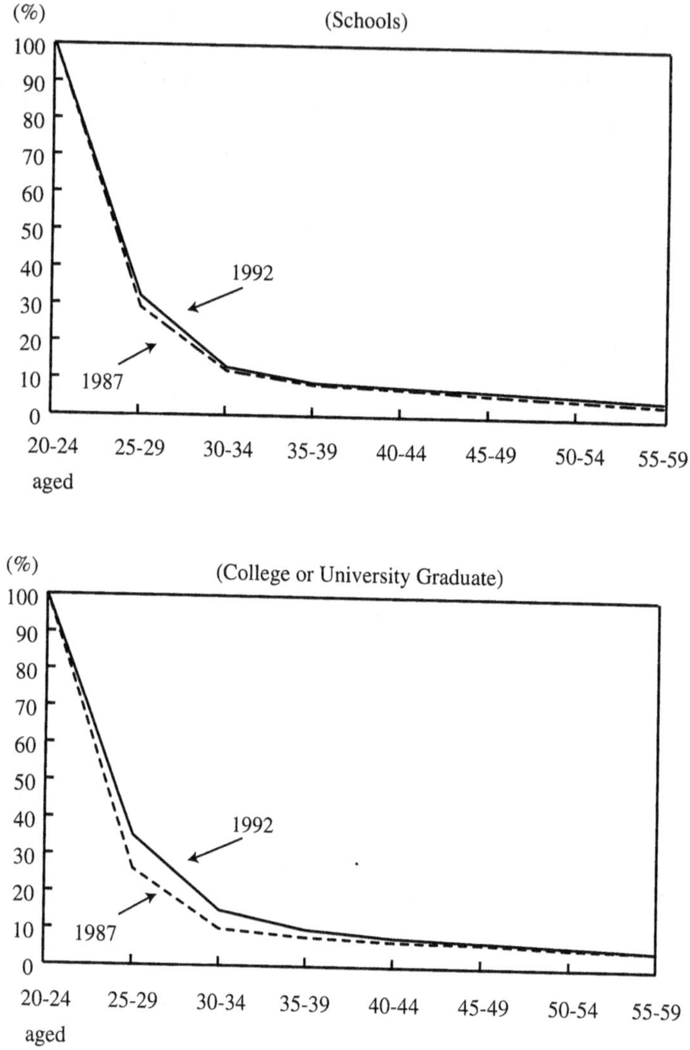

Figure 3-(3)-5. Ratio of continued employment female workers.

Source: Computed on a trial basis by the Labor Economy Section, Ministry of Labor, *Basic Survey on Wage Structure*

Note: Factors are as follows:

$K_{a+5} = A \times K_a$

$$A = \frac{L_{a+5.4} \text{ (Over 5 years of continuous management)}}{L_{a\,62} \text{ (Total of continuous management)}}$$

K_a: No. of continued employment workers by age group, ($K_{20-24} = 100$)

$L_{a\,62}$: No.of workers by age group, in 1987

$L_{a+5.4}$: No.of workers over 5 years of continued employment than age group, by 5 years in 1992

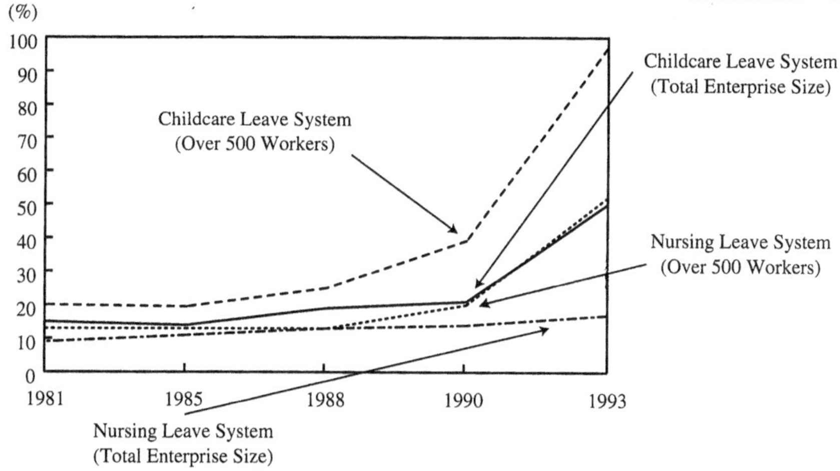

Figure 3-(8)-6. Proportion of enterprises establishing childcare leave system and nursing leave system.

Source: Ministry of Labor, Status on Operation of Protection of Women (1981, 1985), Basic Survey on Female Workers Employment Management (1988,1998).

Sweden

Ann Numhauser-Henning

1. GOVERNMENT POLICIES AIMING AT HARMONISING WORKING LIFE AND FAMILY LIFE

A. In General. On the Necessity of Systems to Support the Equal Employment Opportunities Act

The government has only recently expressed its policies about equal opportunities for men and women in a Bill for the Parliament, proposing some changes in the 1991 Equal Opportunities Act as well in the existing social scheme for subsidised parental leaves[1] The bill summons up the results of the 1988 five-year plan on equality measures.[2]

The 1988 plan focused on labour-market and educational issues and also contained goals and measures in relation to women's participation within the economy and family life. Aiming at promoting equality in the long-term perspective as well as furthering the general ambitions, the outcome was not a total success – changes come slowly. With regard to labour-market participation Sweden has a very high average employment rate, almost as high among women as among men. In 1993 the employed amounted to 72.6% of the active population (that is, people from 16 to 64 years of age), 72.1% of the women as compared to 73% of the men. Due to recession, the employment rates have been falling somewhat since 1990, when the average employment rate reached 82.4%. The differences between men and women have decreased, though, and is now less than 1%. And, with respect to unemployment rates, among women they amounted to 6.6% and among men to 9.7 in 1993, the average being 8.2%. Until 1986 unemployment rates were always higher among women than among men.[3] Nevertheless, women are very unevenly distributed over the labour-market and there are essential differences with regard to pay, etc. These differences are partly explained by women working part-time in low-ranked jobs, but wage differences of 1–8% are considered to be of a pure discriminatory nature.[4]

The governmental conclusion is that despite the formal obstacles for equality among men and women essentially having been abolished, in Swedish society there is still a considerable lack of equality in practice. The government states that the goal for public policies within the area remains the same as before: to assure women and men of equal rights, responsibilities and possibilities within every es-

---

1. Prop. 1993/94:147 om jämställdhetspolitiken, Delad makt, Delat ansvar (Shared power, shared responsibility), Stockholm 1994.
2. Prop. 1987/88:105 om jämställdhetspolitiken inför 90-talet, Stockholm 1988.
3. *See* further Statistical Yearbook of 1994, The Central Bureau of Statistics (SCB), Stockholm 1994.
4. *See* further SOU 1993:7, Löneskillnader och lönediskriminering (Wage Differences and Wage Discrimination), Stockholm 1993.

sential area of life. Changes demand goal-oriented activities to achieve an even distribution of power and influences, equal possibilities to reach economic independence, equal opportunities in working life, equal opportunities in education and personal development, equal responsibilities concerning housework and children, and, the abolition of sex-related violence in the society. The achievement of these goals requires public measures within different parts of society, concludes the government. Propositions and decisions in any political area of society, and especially educational, labour-market, business and social-policy issues, must be analysed from an equal-opportunities perspective.[5] Apart from reforms and activities dealt with further on in this paper, a number of activities have been or will be carried out in different fields to promote these goals. As was already mentioned, in 1991 a new Equal Opportunities Act was introduced – partly to meet with the, at that time future, requirements of the EEA-agreement, that now has come about, and an eventual membership in the European Union (EU), but also to overcome some weaknesses in the 1979 Act. Further on, special funding has been offered for equality promoting measures in higher education as well as to support research in this field. Special labour-market-policy means are offered men or women being employed in and/or introduced in non-traditional professions. The granting of regional industry subsidies requests at least 40% men and 40% women among the new hirings. A special Business-Life Academy is to be introduced to stimulate the appointment of women deputies. On a regional basis, every County Board (Länsstyrelse) should have a special official, who is an expert on equality among the sexes. When sports are funded, equality issues are also focused upon. And, finally, regarding the 1994 elections, most parties made it a rule, that every second name on the lists should be that of a woman.

The governmental policies declared in the 1993/94 bill on equality is the declaration of a conservative-liberal government. The Liberal party especially has been known to be very active in promoting equality issues. When the first Swedish Equal Opportunities Act was introduced in 1979, the Government was a liberal one, and the act was introduced despite the opposition of the social-democratic party and the unions, among others. The critics did not, however, disagree on the importance of promoting equality issues as such, only on doing so by legislation in the chosen form. Furthermore, during the 1980s these differences seem to have diminished, and there are small or no differences concerning equality policies in general as expressed in the 1988 five-year plan earlier referred to, presented by a social democratic government, and the current bill. About family policies there are some political differences of importance, though. Only recently the Government passed a proposition on 'Vårdnadsbidrag' (Child-Care Support) through parliament with the support of a small part of the opposition – the New Democrats – a reform the social democrats have promised to abolish should they win the elections in September 1994.[6] The parliament has also recently passed a reform concerning the existing social security scheme on parental leave, granting one of the totally 12 subsidised months exclusively to the father.[7] However, this reform was supported by both the social democrats and the left, but not by the New Democrats. Apart from these differences, what most of all threatens furthered equality is economic recession and the general crisis of the Swedish welfare society.

---

5. Prop. 1993/94:147 pp. 14 *et seq*. With regard to recent developments, *see* also Investigations Committee Directive 1994:124.
6. *See* further Sec. 2.C below.
7. *See* further Sec. 1.C and 2.C below.

B. Women's Participation from the Perspective of Human Resource Policies

In more recent equality-policies documents the general policies on equality issues are motivated not only by means of justice, but also by quality means. The importance of utilising the competence of women as well as men is frequently stressed in relation to economic growth and quality in working life *per se.*[8] In recent reforms of the higher education system, the importance of enforcing equality among the sexes within the universities in order to promote quality in education and science has been especially pointed out.[9]

The interest for human-resource-management policies in general has been growing – in Sweden as elsewhere – during the last decade or so, this being the natural outcome of technical developments, Service Society and more flexible work patterns. Despite the importance that is given from this perspective, not only to developing the skills and flexibility of the employee, but also to the creation of a working environment that is satisfactory not only from a physical but also psychological point of view, and the importance of both sexes being present at the work place to achieve this, women still meet with special difficulties in employment-practices. Employers suppose that women take on the heaviest part of child care and the like, thus, creating more problems in organising work – and they are not entirely wrong.[10]

Of course there is the 1991 Equal Opportunities Act to deal with this. To promote equality the new Act contains, not only rules prohibiting the discrimination in individual employment decisions, but also reinforcing rules on active measures to promote employment of both sexes. Thus, the Act states an obligation for employers with ten employees or more to make up a special Equality Plan for the company on an annual basis including, for instance, recruitment issues. Recently, a demand was added to the Equality Plan that this must contain thorough statistics about the wages paid to men and women respectively.[11] The prohibition on discrimination in hiring in the Swedish Act, however, requires the possibility of a comparison between applicants of both sexes – that is discrimination against a woman can only be considered in the case where a man is hired. Thus the Swedish Act, as it stands, does not meet with the requirements of the Council Directive 76/207/EEC, according to the Court of Justice of the European Communities in the so-called Dekker Case (177/88), where the Court declared it direct discrimination to deny a pregnant women employment on the grounds of pregnancy, irrespective of whether there was a male applicant or not. For the time being, it can not be denied that pregnant women – or even women who supposedly will have children in the near future – may have special difficulties in getting a job. It has also been reported in the media, that the recent changes in the 1982 Employment Protection Act regarding dismissal due to shortage of work, are being utilised in a discriminatory manner. In these cases the last-in-first-out principle apply. However, according to the reform, the employer has the right to choose two employees of special importance for the company at his free will, before applying the principle.[12] It seems that this rule in a number of cases has been used to give preference to more recently hired employees, firing, in particular, pregnant women or women with small children.

8. *See*, for instance, Prop 1993/94:147 p. 15. and p. 67.
9. Prop. 1992/93:169 and 170.
10. Cf. below Secs. 1.C and 2.C.
11. Prop. 1993/94:147 and SFS 1994:292.

C. Social Assistance with Regard to the Caring for Children and Ageing Parents

The main difference in time occupation between Swedish men and women emerges when there are children. Women's paid work diminishes and is partly substituted by non-paid housework, while men continue their wage work as before the child was born. Thus, according to a study carried out by the SCB in 1990–91, on average women's paid work amounts to 27 hours weekly and their unpaid house work to 33 hours weekly, while men's paid work amounts to 41 hours as compared to 20 hours of un-paid house work.[13] 'The Tacit Contract' between women and men seems to imply that women support full-time paid work for men by part-time work and household 'duty', thus, to a considerable extent remaining economically dependent.

The goal of both family and equality policies is to see to it that women and men can combine parenthood and practical child care with paid work.[14] According to the government, there is now a growing awareness of the importance of both parents sharing the practical responsibilities for home and children.[15] Nevertheless, despite the goal expressed in the 1988 equality plan – that by the end of 1993 one third of the fathers of small children should make use of the subsidised parental leave – in 1992, still, only 9% of the subsidies were paid to fathers.[16] In order to speed up the desired development, as from the 1st of July, 1994, one out of twelve subsidised months of parental leave is exclusive to the father (*see* further, Sec. 2.C.). Also of great importance for the real possibility to combine parenthood and paid work, is not only the rights to parental leave but also the services for nursing children in general. In order to strengthen these possibilities the parliament has decided that, from 1995, it is a municipal obligation to offer child care services for children 12 months of age or more, to meet with the actual demand.[17]

The general policies concerning the care of the elderly (that is ageing parents) will be touched upon below in Sections 2.C and D.

2. EXISTING SCHEMES FOR HARMONISING WORKING LIFE AND FAMILY LIFE

A.B. Reduction in Working Time, Flexible Working Schedules, Part-Time

The legal standpoint regarding working time according to Swedish law is that the quantity of hours to be performed in an employment depends on what the parties involved have agreed upon, while the scheduling of the agreed quantity of working hours is regarded as part of the employer's managerial prerogatives.[18] To begin with, there were hardly any limitations, but in due course the permitted maximum of work-

12. Cf. prop. 1993/94:67. The new rules apply as of the 1 of January 1994. However, the new Government has only recently put forward a bill restoring, among other things, the former seniority rules of the 1982 Act, *see* prop. 1994/95:76. These 'new' rules are supposed to be applied as of the 1 of January 1995.
13. I tid och otid, report nr 79, 1992, SCB.
14. Prop. 1993/94:147 p 66.
15. Prop. 1993/94:147 p. 15.
16. In 1988 the figure was 6.5%.
17. Prop. 1993/94:11, rskr. 1993/94:117.
18. Cf., for instance, AD 1960:20, 1968:9 and 1984:108.

ing hours was regulated by law[19] and some restrictions were put forward on, for instance, rest time, breaks, weekly holidays, vacation and so on, but also in the form of a right to reduced hours for parental leave.[20]

Regarding the amount of regular working hours, according to the current Swedish working-hours legislation, the 1982 Working Hours Act,[21] regular working hours may not exceed 40 hours a week. If necessary, with regard to the special nature or conditions of the job concerned, the regular working hours may be 40 hours a week on an average for four weeks. However, the 1982 Act is not compelling but may be overridden – or partly completed – by collective agreements at the national federation level.[22] The regulations thus offer a legal framework of considerable flexibility. Normally, collective agreements stipulate the regular working hours for full-time employment as well as conditions for overtime work, leaving it to the individuals themselves to reach an agreement with their employer on, for instance part-time work.[23] As was already mentioned, apart from these rules, the disposition of working hours is – in principle – part of the managerial prerogatives. However, according to the Act the employer has a duty to notify employees, if possible, at least two weeks in advance of any alteration in the disposition of regular working hours. Important changes also call for primary negotiations and the changes must not – without the employee's consent – go beyond the original employment agreement, that might include also scheduling issues.[24]

The 40-hour week was introduced in Sweden in 1971–73, and since then there have been no other statutory changes in the regular annual working time except the introduction of the fifth week of annual vacation in 1978. The decrease in hours actually worked has been taken in other ways, mainly in the form of increased – legally based – absenteeism and individually agreed part-time employments. Most of the unions agree that working hours should be further reduced, but opinions differ as to how extensively and rapidly this can be accomplished, what alternative forms should be chosen, and how the reductions are to be financed. The six-hours-day-five-days-a-week model for a long time was the top priority goal for the unions – especially the Central Organisation of Salaried Employees (the TCO) and the Swedish Confederation of Trade Unions (the LO) – the reason being that this solution promotes the combination of wage-work and family life and thereby favours equality between the sexes, as well as counteracting disability in working life and hence the marginalization of workers. It also has been considered as supporting union, political and idealistic work of different types, thus promoting political democracy. However, already the 1986 LO congress declared this model a non-realistic goal, giving priority to selectively shortened hours for shift workers and the parents of

19. In 1919 the first Working Hours Act was introduced in Sweden, establishing the 48-hour week.
20. *See* further Sec. 2.C.
21. The Act applies to employees in general with the exception of home-workers, employees in leading positions or in positions of trust, those employed in the employer's household and ship-employment. The Act does not pay attention to the employee having two or more employments by different employers, though.
22. The rules on overtime, additional time and night-rest may also be waived by a collective agreement at the local level (valid for up to one month). Such local agreements may not be practised on a permanent basis, though.
23. Occasionally, the collective agreement contains compelling rules regarding the allowed minimum of working hours, since social-welfare rules do not apply to people with very short working-hours, i.e. less than 17 hours a week. It may also list permitted types of part-time employment. In the State sector, part-time jobs must – in principle – amount to at least 40% of full-time (Sec. 7 SFS 1989:166).
24. Cf. AD 1979:66.

small children, also considering a sixth week of annual vacation for everybody as an important reform. The Swedish Professional Workers Confederation (the SACO/SR), too, has abandoned the six-hour-day goal and opposes in general further legislation as regards working hours, giving priority to negotiated solutions and individual choice. The employer's side generally objects to shortened working hours but promotes systems with more flexibility, and preferably on an individual basis. Among the political parties, opinions differ.[25] This discussion mostly took place in the 1980s, however. Lately, and due to recession, there has been little said about shortened hours.[26] The governmental Working Time Investigations Committee, initiated in 1987 to investigate precisely the consequences of alternative ways to shorten working hours, came to the conclusion that there was no room – nor wellfounded need[27] – for statutory reforms aiming at shortened working hours. In the report, the Committee stipulated general goals for a future working-time policy and supported the idea of increased flexibility in the scheduling of regular working time. Later on, another investigations committee put forward the proposal that the 40-hours working week in the 1982 Act should be exchanged for a rule on the corresponding annual working time, thus giving room for compressed working weeks, etc.[28] As for this proposal, quite some time has already passed since the committee published its findings, one of the reasons for the passivity on behalf of the legislator being the developments with regard to working-time issues within the European Community. The Council Directive 93/104/EEC on the organisation of working time is much more restrictive and detailed than the future Swedish regulation of working time was suggested to be (and even than the current 1982 Act is). In Sweden working hours are again the object for an investigation's committee.[29]

Nevertheless, as was indicated above, the 1982 Act as it stands authorises the parties to completely – or only in certain parts – override the statutory rules by means of a collective agreement. Almost every collective agreement has its special rules regarding working time (often in a rather complicated way related to the wage system) and we can find a variety of regulations. In the important metal-work sector within the LO, for instance, we find an example of the annual working-time rule – the agreement stating a regular working time of 40 (or less in shift work) hours a week on an average for a period of one year. In the private white-collar sector, on the other hand, according to the general agreement, regular working hours amount to 40 hours a week on average for a period of four weeks, but both the number of regular working hours and the averaging period may be regulated otherwise by local collective agreements. Nevertheless, there is a considerable uniformity about the scheduling of regular full-time working hours on the Swedish labour market. Thus, according to an investigation, 86% of all work was performed in normal day-time (07–18) and

---

25. *See*, for instance, SOU 1989:53.
26. In Sweden, reforms regarding shortened working hours – whether on a general or o selective basis – have rarely been seen as ways to combat unemployment, but as means to promote welfare and equality among different groups in society. It seems, though, that the LO for the coming year will demand a reduction in working-time with 100 hours a year precisely to counteract unemployment.
27. According to the committee, none of six possible reforms implying shortened working hours was socially or economically acceptable; the supply of labour would decrease, educational facilities would be overstrained, urbanisation trends accentuated, the economy rendered more sluggish, private consumption curtailed and taxes raised. Furthermore, the organisation of labour would be hampered, inconvenient and irregular scheduling increased, and joint leisure activities prevented, SOU 1989:53.
28. SOU 1992:27, Årsarbetstid (Annual working time), Stockholm 1992.
29. *See* Investigation's Committee Directive 1994:99.

56% of the employees were only involved in day-time work Monday to Friday, while 5% of all work was performed during weekends and only 1% during nights.[30] And, despite the predominance of general regulations on working hours of the type described, a recent investigation also showed that as a result of general or local agreements on scheduling and so on, no less than 42% of the active population had certain possibilities to choose their daily working time. These possibilities were very unevenly distributed throughout the labour market. Thus, they were available to 20% in the LO sector, 50% in the TCO sector, 66% in the SACO/SR sector and 80% of the self-employed.[31]

Flexibility meaning 'reduced working hours' has traditionally been a demand expressed by the trade-unions. Demands for increased flexibility concerning the scheduling of working time are nowadays just as often voiced by the employer's side as by the employee's. Flexibility is then relating to that process which is aimed at promoting adaptation to new conditions that arise as a result of changing structures in production and in market economy. Flexibility in this newer sense, expelled as 'inconvenient' hours and – most of all – part-time work, however, is also seen as related to demands from an increased number of women in the working population.

The high rate of part-time work may be considered one of the main characteristics of the Swedish labour market. Thus, the part-time rate is about 25%, about 85% of the part-timers being women. In fact about 45% of all women in the Swedish labour market work part-time. The increase in women's employment mainly took place in the 1970s, and part-time employment increased steadily until the mid-1980s. However, the current trend is that part-time work is slightly decreasing. There is also a strong tendency towards longer part-time.

An important ingredient in this development is of course – in principle – the unrestricted right to part-time arrangements in Sweden. Furthermore, part-time work has undoubtedly been supported by different types of statutory regulations and reforms. There is no general legislation on part-time work except for the rules on restricted right to additional time in the 1982 Working Hours Act.[32] As was already indicated above, part-time employment is normally agreed upon individually by the employer and the employee involved, though it may come about as reduced hours in full-time employment. According to the Act on Parental Leave, there is a statutory regulated right to reduced hours for the parents of small children. The possibilities of taking part-time retirement, from 61 years of age onwards, also promote part-time work, and so do other rules which form part of the social security system.

The legal background implies that there is a great variety in part-time employment arrangements throughout the labour market. However, as it was already indicated, most part-time workers are women, and today's typical pattern has been described as follows: 'Women increasingly tend to hold full-time jobs up to the birth of the first child and while being on parental leave. When returning to work, after about one year of parental leave, they tend to change from full time to part time. Then, women predominantly remain employed on a part-time basis during the years of childbearing and birth of additional children. When children start school mothers increasingly extend their working hours to full time'.[33] From the beginning – during the 1970s – there was a pressure from unions and employees on employers to create

30. SOU 1989:53.
31. SOU 1989:53.
32. Rules easy to circumvent, temporarily taking on a full-time employment.
33. Sundström, A Study in the Growth of Part-time Work in Sweden, Stockholm 1987 p 11 *et seq.*

part-time jobs.[34] These became exceptionally frequent in the public sector, which was the expanding sector during the period concerned and employed lots of women. Afterwards the many part-time jobs have become an obstacle for women employees wanting to work more hours. Legally stipulated rights to reduced hours in part-time employment often is enough for women's needs, whereas, from the employer's point of view, part-time employees offer a certain flexibility accepting overtime/additional time or full-time jobs on occasion.[35]

C. Parental Leaves, Child-Care Leaves and Leaves for Caring for Frail Elderly Parents

The high rates of absenteeism[36] – though legally supported – are to a large extent enforced by the development of the structures in the Swedish labour market, mainly the high rates of employment. When practically everybody is working, there is an absolute need (which has both personal and societal implications) for leave of absence for various reasons. Since the early 1970s there has been a trend towards granting the employee a right to leave of absence – not only in cases of illness, public duties, etc. – but also in situations that more clearly involve a balancing of personal interest on the one hand and wage-work on the other.

The 1978 Act on Parental Leave replaces previous legislation which dated back to 1939 and contained prohibitions against giving notice to, or dismissing, pregnant women as well as rules concerning the right to some leave of absence in connection with the birth of a child. In the 1978 Act, the right to leave of absence in order to care for a child was extended to a considerable degree; since 1974, such a leave of absence is also to a certain extent combined with the right to receive a so-called parental allowance according to the 1962 Act on National Insurance. During 1994 there has been a number of changes as well in the 1978 Act as in the 1962 Act, mainly due to the introduction of the special, so called Child-Care Support. The Child-Care Support is a monthly allowance of 2000 crowns (approximately US $ 275), paid to the parents of children 1–3 years of age.[37]

The child-care leave during the child's first year is – in principle[38] – paid for by the social security scheme according to Chapter 4 of the 1962 Act on National Insurance. Until only recently there was a right to leave of absence with full pay – the allowance amounted to 90% of the employee's gross income – for 360 days and another 90 days with a guarantee-pay of 60 Swedish crowns a day until the child reached the age of eight.[39] With the introduction of the Child-Care Support, how-

34. Rising real wages, separate taxation, rising marginal taxes, expanded public child-care facilities as well as the design of social benefits greatly increased the profitability of paid (part-time) work as compared to household work during the 1970s.
35. According to Sundström, the driving forces for both the rise in part-time jobs and their decline from 1983 onwards are to be found on the supply-side of the labour market.
36. In respect of the rates of absenteeism the right to annual holiday is the most important. Second in importance is absenteeism based on illness and third, parental leave.
37. The Act (1994:553) on Child-Care Support, entering into force on the 1st of July 1994. Cf. also sec. 1A. – Since this report was completed (in June 1994), the new Government has fulfilled its former declarations putting forward a bill to the parliament that the right to Child-Care Support shall be abolished as from the 1 of January 1995, *see* prop. 1994/95:61.
38. As will be touched upon below, the right to allowance includes a quite high degree of flexibility, and there is no obligation whatsoever to actually use it during the child's first year.
39. The time for parental leave was extended from 12 to 15 months from the 1 of July 1989.

ever, this time was reduced to 360 days.[40] Because of the Swedish economic crisis, the allowance has also been reduced from 90% of the employee's gross income to only 80%, with the exception of 60 days during which the allowance still amounts to 90%.[41]

The right to allowance includes a certain degree of flexibility. It may be used for total leave or as reduced hours (by a quarter of a day or half a day). In the latter case, the leave will be of a considerable duration.

In accordance with current views regarding the equality between the sexes, this right comprises women and men alike.[42] Since the use was not very equally distributed, though,[43] within the recent reform there were some changes made. According to the rules, the mother and the father have a right to 180 days allowance each. However, if they want to they can transfer this right to the other parent, with the exception of 30 days (being the ones paid for by 90% of the gross income)[44] This reform, thus, more or less obliges the father to take at least his 30 days off – in the other case leaving the family with only 330 days of child-care allowance – a consequence considered of great importance for the promotion of equality policies. – Of course, if there is only one parent (or the other one is sick or disabled), this parent has the right to the complete 360-days allowance.

In addition, there is a right to paid leave for a maximum of 120 days a year per child in connection with the child's sickness, as well as a right to paid leave for two days a year for contacts with schools and the like and a special right for fathers to paid leave for ten days when the child is born. These rules apply until the child is 12 years of age, and the temporary parental allowance can be transferred from the parent of the child to another person – for instance a grand-mother or a friend – actually taking a leave of absence from paid employment to care for the sick child.

According to the 1978 Act on Parental Leave – regulating the right to leave of absence (but not to pay) vis á vis the employer – there is now a right for the employee to full-time leave of absence until the child is 3 years of age.[45] Apart from this, and the right to leave whenever receiving parental allowance according to the 1962 Act, the 1978 Act comprises rules on the right to shorter working days (without pay) for employees with children under the age of eight years. An employee has the right to work three quarters of full-time (normally six hours a day) during these years and then go back to full-time again, that is without losing their basic full-time employment.[46]

---

40. SFS 1994:554. The above mentioned governmental proposition on an abolishment of the right to Child-Care Support includes the reinstatement of the right to 90 days with guarantee-pay, prop. 1994/95:61.
41. These new rules apply from the 1st of January 1995, and only to the care of children born from this date onwards. – As a matter of fact, the 1962 Act applies to all parents irrespectively of having an employment or not. The parental allowance, normally being related to income, in these cases is paid as a guarantee of 64 crowns (about US $ 8) a day.
42. Of course, both parents must not receive compensation at the same time.
43. In 1992, only 9% of the total amount of parent-allowence days paid for, were used by fathers. However, in the beginning of the 1990s 38% of all married fathers and 44% of the fathers living together with the child's mother without being married, took some leave to care for the child during its first year, Prop. 1993/94:147 p. 68 *et seq*.
44. SFS 1994:605.
45. SFS 1994:555. Until the introduction of the Child-Care Support, this right amounted only to 18 months. – According to the above mentioned governmental bill putting an end to the right to Child-Care Support, 18 months is again to be the rule, prop. 1994/95:61.
46. According to AD 1982:96, an employee with reduced hours is to be considered a 'full-time employee' with regard to employment benefits in general.

As for the scheduling of parental leave, the main rule is that the employer must be given two months advance notice, except concerning the temporary care of sick children. Leave must be given on the day requested by the employee and reduction of working hours must, in principle, be distributed throughout the working week. If an agreement on scheduling a reduction cannot be reached, the decision rests with the employer, but reduction must regard the beginning or the end of the day.

According to the 1978 Act, the right to leave of absence for child-care is – in principle[47] – conditioned by a qualifying period of employment of at least six months. If not employed for such a time, only women employees have a right to six weeks leave before and six weeks after delivery. This rule is expected to be changed in the short future, though, to adjust to the Council Directive 92/85/EEC on the introduction of measures to encourage improvements in the safety and health at work of pregnant workers and workers who have recently given birth or are breastfeeding. This directive states no special time of employment to qualify for the rights according to the directive, and guarantees a leave amounting to at least 14 weeks totally before and after a delivery. An investigations committee has already put forward a proposal for a new Act on Parental Leave, considering the rights of pregnant employees and employees who have recently given birth or are breastfeading according to the directive only just mentioned. The proposal also considers a change in the right of pregnant women to be transferred to other responsibilities. According to the current Act on Parental Leave – in case it is needed and possible to arrange – such a right to transfer exists only for 60 days before expected delivery.[48] The future act is suggested to give such a right during pregnancy as well as breastfeeding whenever a transfer is needed.[49]

The Act on Parental Leave is compulsory insofar as it is to the advantage of the employee; hence it must not be signed away. However, it is rather common for collective agreements to contain rules on further rights. For instance, in the municipal sector, the right to reduced hours without pay for the parents of infant children is extended to comprise children up to 12 years of age. Many agreements have extended the period of right to re-employment after a collective dismissal (normally one year) in cases of parental leave, and so on.

Regarding social-policy schemes for children, it should be mentioned that in Sweden there is also a general Child allowance, paid on a monthly basis to every child until the age of sixteen.[50] With regard to children of separated parents, there is also the maintenance-advance institution.[51] Both can be considered forms of contributing to the upkeep and upbringing of children – in the latter case in so-called incomplete families – and the same amount is being paid to all children regardless of family-incomes.[52]

In 1988 a right to temporary paid leave for the care of severely ill closely related persons was introduced.[53] The payment amounts to 80% of the sickness ben-

47. This condition does not apply to leaves in case of the child's sickness, cf. above.
48. In case working conditions constitute a risk for the health or safety of the pregnant women and a transfer is not possible, there is a right to a special allowance during a maximum of 50 days for the pregnant women within 60 days of expected delivery according to the 1962 Act on National Insurance.
49. SOU 1994:41, Ledighetslagstiftningen – en översyn (Statutory Leave of Absence – a Survey), Stockholm 1994.
50. The General Child Allowances Act (1947:529).
51. The Maintenance Advances Act (1964:143).
52. The Child allowance increases with the number of children, though. *See* further, for instance Lavin-Westerhäll, Support of Families with Children in Swedish Welfare Law, Lund 1985.
53. The (1988:1465) Act on allowance and leave for the caring of closely related persons.

efits during a maximum of 60 days a year[54] – with regard to persons with HIV/AIDS the allowance can be paid for 240 days, though. The allowance is financed through the Social Insurance, but the Act includes rules on the right to a corresponding leave of absence from employment. Thus, the allowance is paid to persons taking a leave of absence to temporarily care for a closely related person that is very ill. The care must take place in a private home. There are no specified rules on the relationship required, and the rules do not only apply to family or relatives. As a matter of fact, any person taking a leave of absence to care for another in such a situation is supposed to be close enough. As in other cases, the allowance may be used for a total leave or as reduced hours (by a quarter of a day or half a day).

Except for this right, which only applies when a person is very ill – more or less in a final stage – there are in Swedish labour law, no legal rights for an employee to a leave of absence for caring for frail or sick elderly parents. Further rights to leave than those legally stipulated, may be granted by collective agreements. Such rules normally relate to the severe illness of a close relative, much like the one provided for in the 1988 Act just described. Taking care of elderly parents on a more lengthy basis, on the other hand, calls for an agreement with the employer. The official view is that old people are not the responsibility of their grown-up children, but of society – cf. further below.

D. Public Services or Systems for Nursing Children or Caring Frail Elderly Parents

The development of societal service facilities for child nursing and the like is a condition for women's participation in working life. The expansion of such systems, like day-care centres and family-day-care schemes for children from the age of 1 year (or even six months) up to the age of 7, as well as after-school centres for children 7–12 years started out already in the 1970s. Only in December 1993, however, the parliament imposed an obligation on the municipalities to provide child-care facilities for children 1–12 years of age, to meet the actual demand at the latest in 1995. The rules are included in the 1980 Social Services Act.[55] The obligation applies to the children of working parents as well as to those with unemployed parents seeking jobs and student-parents. There are public as well as private day-care centres, and those operating on a co-operative basis. The financing system is mainly the same in all these cases, the cost being paid partly by public subsidies and partly by fees paid by the parents according to their economic possibilities. The rules are to some extent co-ordinated with the new rules on Child-Care Support.[56] Thus, the Child-Care Support is reduced in case the child receives care partially paid for by public means.[57] According to a recent survey by the SCB, 430 000 children below the age of 7 were attended in some kind of day-care centres by the end of 1993, and another 68.000 were queuing up.[58] Apart from the day-care

54. SFS 1994:318. This rule applies as of the 1 of July 1994 – earlier the right amounted to 30 days, only.
55. SFS 1994:11.
56. Cf. above Sec. 2.C. – Beware that the government is now doing away with the right to Child-Care Support all together, prop. 1994/95:61.
57. The normally 2000 crowns are reduced to 1.350 crowns if the child is taken care of not more than 15 hours a week and to 700 crowns when looked after 16–30 hours a week. For children in full-time care, there is no right to Child-Care Support.
58. Cf. the daily newspaper Sydsvenska Dagbladet, 21 of June 1994.

centres there are family-day-care homes, both on a public and a private basis.

With regard to the elderly, the demographic situation of Sweden has been changing, as in all of Europe, the most significant characteristic being the increase of the elderly population. This increase, especially relating to the very oldest, and its resulting higher median age, has put a significant burden on health and medical care especially concerning the needs and demands for health and medical care services. Providing health care is – like child care – a responsibility for the local governments, now according to the 1982 Health and Medical Care Act, having the obligation to offer health care to all those who are residing within their jurisdiction. Medical care is primarily provided for by 26 regional and local authorities,[59] but all the local municipalities have a responsibility of certain medical care, especially for elderly people. Although this public authority responsibility does not exclude private providers, the health care system in Sweden may be characterised as being primarily public and part of a universal health insurance system. The costs are financed by revenues from employer charges, with the patients paying a minimal fee for service. Also most private practitioners are included in this system, and patients pay substantially the same fee for private medical care as they would for public care.[60] As was already indicated, the local governments are responsible for certain medical care, and here we should note the medical care and supervision of homes for the aged and service homes, also provided for by the local government. Apart from these, the local governments, through social welfare authorities, offer service for elderly people living at home in accordance with the 1980 Social Services Act. These services consist of, for instance, shopping, house-cleaning, cooking and personal services of all kinds, and are partly paid for by fees in accordance with the individual's income, but otherwise by public means. As the results of economic crisis, galloping public expenses and cutbacks in the medical care system, lately we have seen a development that forces a growing number of elderly people to stay in their homes, requiring more and more advanced personal services, including medical care.

Nevertheless, a recently published survey, carried out by the National Social Welfare Board (Socialstyrelsen), shows that the majority of elderly Swedish people are fairly healthy, and they agree with the public policies to give priority to public care systems. According to the survey, in case they would need care on a more regular basis, 86% of the elderly prefer public care services to help within the family.[61]

3. CONCLUDING REMARKS

The current Swedish working-hours regulation (through legislation and general collective agreements) gives us a regular annual working time in full-time industrial employment of 1,796 hours, longer than in most other European countries, but shorter than in Japan and in the USA.[62] In spite of this, the actual annual working time in

59. 23 landstingskommuner and 3 municipalities throughout Sweden.
60. On the Swedish medical care system, *see*, for instance, Westerhäll, Medical Law, An Introduction, Stockholm 1994.
61. 8% prefers care provided by a family member and 2% other private providers, *see* further Socialstyrelsen, Äldre i Sverige och Europa, Ädelutvärderingen 93:4, Stockholm 1993.
62. The regular annual working time is based on the 40-hours week, taking into account public holidays and five weeks of annual vacation.

Sweden among employed persons, 1,482 hours, is shorter than in most countries.[63] This is mainly due to the two main characteristics of the Swedish labour market – the high degree of part-time employment, on the one hand, and absenteeism on the other – both being related to the high occupational rates in general, and especially to the large proportion of working women.

The fact that the occupational rate among women is almost as high as among men, is due, not only to equal-opportunities policies in general, but to the existing schemes with regard to the caring for children etc. The social insurance is mainly built on benefits compensating lost income. It is thus fundamental, also for women, to see to it that they have got an employment – or at least a registered income – before they start to build up a family.

In general, the outcome of the system is reflected in Swedish birth-rates, which are the highest in Europe together with Irish women, or 2,1 child per woman.

As described above, there have been some changes made in the existing schemes lately. Especially the new Child-Care Support has been criticised from an equal-opportunities perspective, the critics stating that this right to a monthly support until the child reaches 3 years of age, is likely to keep women off the labour market to a growing extent. Long leaves-of-absence in combination with very high unemployment rates in general will make women's reintegration into the labour market increasingly difficult. At the same time the amount of support is too low, making women more economically dependent on their husbands. As was already indicated above, the social democrats have declared their intention to abolish this new Support when, and if, they win the elections in September 1994.[64]

However, with regard to the system as a whole, the disputes on the Child-Care Support seem to be only a minor issue. What seems more threatening, are the cut-backs in the social insurance scheme in general due to economic crisis. Furthermore, economic crisis and the crisis of the Welfare system as such constitute a special threat to the employment of women per se, since women make up the majority of the employees in the public sector. In this perspective it seems increasingly important to pursue the public goals concerning equal rights for men and women, not least with regard to an even distribution of power and influences.[65]

---

63. From SOU 1989:53, report number 6 by Lars-Olof Pettersson.
64. This promise has now been kept, the Government presenting a bill to Parliament on the abolishment of the right to Child-Care Support as from the 1st of January 1995, prop. 1994/95:61.
65. As a result of the 1994 elections women increased their representation in the Swedish Parliament considerably, the number of women being now more than 40%!

United Kingdom

Alan C. Neal

INTRODUCTION[1]

The meeting of working life with family life has, of course, been an issue of concern since the dawn of time, however one defines 'working life' or 'family life'. Both are a direct result of the organisational imperative consequent upon the development of 'social life', and lie at the foundation of 'societies' and their effective survival. However, the nature and potential consequences of perceived conflicts between these two aspects of societal activity in modern industrialised States have led to a renewed concern amongst politicians, legislators, lawyers, and a wide variety of social interest groups about some of the negative effects of an incompatibility between the two spheres of activity.

Some of this concern has been motivated by what are seen as trends towards the fragmentation and weakening of 'the family', as an assumed 'basic building block' in the organisational fabric of most such States. Concern has also been stimulated by widely promoted views[2] that 'equal treatment' in all walks of life – particularly, equal treatment and equal opportunities as between women and men – should be a fundamental goal for the modern development of the social structures in such States. Concern about the economic implications of maintaining a 'societal safety net' for increasing numbers of members in those States who are regarded as, in some sense, 'vulnerable' and deserving of protection or special support, has also played a part in bringing such issues to the fore. So, too, have (sometimes dramatic) demographic shifts in the make-up of the population of those States contributed towards this process. Nor should it be forgotten that there is also a significant 'ideological' component in this process – whether this be an adherence to the ideal of the 'Welfare State', an agenda developed out of feminist critiques of existing societal structures, or a socio-economic platform for which the ideology of 'The Market' plays a particularly significant role.

A variety of these stimuli for heightened concern about the compatibility between working life and family life can be identified in the United Kingdom context during the past decade. So, too, have dramatic changes in the British demographic structure, in the appearance of the British labour market, and in the socio-political climate of the United Kingdom during that same period served to make this issue one of immediate and pressing importance.

The following brief presentation raises a selection of issues in the United Kingdom context.[3] Consideration is first given to political-level policy making, in the course of which some basic labour market data and trends are presented. Atten-

1. THE DATA IN THIS REPORT HAS BEEN DRAWN FROM GOVERNMENT STATISTICAL SOURCES AVAILABLE AS OF JULY 1994.
2. Views which, to some eyes, are predicated on an overtly 'patriarchal model'. *Cf.* the problem of 'models, *infra* at note 8.

tion then turns to policy making at the legislative/regulatory level, where it is suggested that the 'models' or 'typologies' used by those concerned with policy development at this level may not adequately reflect the state of family life and working life organisation revealed by recent social and labour market statistics. Against the background thus sketched, consideration is then given to the interface between working life and family life, with particular concentration upon *(i)* children and childcare; *(ii)* working parents; and *(iii)* caring for an ageing population.

UNDERLYING POLICIES TOUCHING UPON WORKING LIFE AND FAMILY LIFE

(I) Policies at the Political Level

Since the arrival in power of a Conservative government under Prime Minister Margaret Thatcher in 1979, a number of fundamental changes have taken place in relation both to social policy at large and to policies concerning working life in particular. Hitherto, the dominant impetus behind such policies – virtually since the end of World War II – had been the ideal of the 'Welfare State', including the model of State social security provision associated with the name of Sir William Beveridge.[4] The years since 1979, however, have witnessed a dramatic shift in emphasis, with policies directed towards a withdrawal of the State from many of its previous interventionist activities and with an ideology firmly wedded to the introduction of the 'discipline of market forces' into areas not only of commercial activity but also in relation to social provision within society.

One particular theme running through many of the stated policies of successive Conservative governments since 1979 has been a re-emphasis upon what are described as 'family values' – a notion which is said by many to reflect a hankering after an idealised vision of Victorian middle-class family life and a slogan around which to assemble a wide variety of measures placing responsibility (economic as well as moral) upon the individual citizen for his own and his family's survival and well-being. Such a theme, however, has been trumpeted against a background of change in British society which has witnessed significant rises in the level of marital breakdowns and divorces, the emergence of large numbers of lone-parent families, and a dramatic shift in balance towards an increasingly aged population.

At the same time, pressures at both a domestic and on an international level have increased the pressure towards enabling women to enter working life and to develop careers in a very different manner from what has earlier been the practice.[5]

---

3. Amongst the issues not addressed in this selective presentation are questions of tax and fiscal policy treatment of family members. Furthermore, there is no more than a passing reference to a range of important matters arising in this context in relation to State social security provision. It should therefore be noted that what is said here does not attempt to deal with important problems of 'personal choices' and individual decisions which may be largely made on the basis of personal economic circumstances.
4. The Report of the Beveridge Committee was published in 1942, and quickly led to the White Papers *Social Insurance Pts. I and II* (Cmd. 6550 and 6551) in 1944.
5. Amongst the more significant pressures from the international level have been those emanating from the institutions of the European Communities, by virtue of the United Kingdom's membership of that body since 1973. This can be seen directly at play in relation to recent legal developments, such as the opinions of the House of Lords in *R. v. Secretary of State for Employment, ex parte Equal Opportunities Commission and another* [1994] I.R.L.R. 176 – declaring that various

Thus, active policies directed towards the promotion of equal opportunities for women in working life and to the elimination of discrimination on the basis of gender have formed a significant feature in recent legislative activity in the field of labour law, and these have been backed by measures to ensure effective implementation of those policies and legal sanctions to encourage employers and others of the seriousness of intent underlying such provisions.[6]

In the British context, too, it has to be remembered that the make-up of the United Kingdom's population now reveals a multi-racial society, with substantial differences in culture and habits manifesting themselves in relation to family life amongst households of differing ethnic backgrounds.[7]

Within this context, it is important to recognise what is nowadays constituted by the notion of 'the family' in the United Kingdom.[8] The available statistics indicate significant changes in recent decades. Thus, for example, the idea that 'the family' will be formed around a stable long-term marital relationship is less prevalent than it was a quarter of a century ago. In particular, divorce features much more significantly than was the case thirty years ago, as can be seen from Table 1.[9] Partly in consequence of this, the proportion of families headed by a lone parent rose dramatically in the period 1971–1992, from 8% to 21% – not only attributable to the increase in families headed by a divorced parent, but also due to a significant increase in the number of families headed by single or separated mothers.[10] Thus, there is something in the order of 1.3 million one-parent families in Great Britain, containing approximately 2.2 million dependent children – a more

---

provisions of domestic British labour law contained in the Employment Protection (Consolidation) Act 1978 were incompatible with,variously, Article 119 of the Treaty of Rome, Council Directive 75/117/EEC, and Council Directive 76/207/EEC – and the enactment of The Sex Discrimination and Equal Pay (Remedies) Regulations 1993 (S.I. 1993 No. 2798) – removing earlier compensation limits in respect of acts of unlawful sex discrimination, in the wake of the judgment of the European Court of Justice in Case C-271/91, *Marshall* v. *Southampton and South-West Hampshire Area Health Authority (No. 2)* [1993] I.R.L.R. 445.

6. It has to be recognised, however, that not all commentators regard this development of active policies backed by effective implementation policies as necessarily reflecting an uncritical acceptance on the part of the United Kingdom of either the specific measures introduced in furtherance of such policies or, even, an unreserved commitment to 'equal opportunities' policies and measures at all. For the purposes of this presentation, however, it suffices to draw attention to the existence of such lack of conviction as to the true motivation of successive British governments.

7. To take just one example, in 1991, some three-quarters of families headed by a Bangladeshi consisted of a married couple with dependent children, by contrast with something in the order of one-third amongst such families headed by a White or a Black person. (*Social Trends 24*, (HMSO London 1994), p. 36 and Table 2.7). *See infra* at note 7. *See* also the literature on ethnic minority women at work, including survey data in C.Brown & P. Gray, *Racial Discrimination: 17 Years after the Act* (pSI, London 1985) and D. Owen & A. Green, 'Labour Market Experience and Occupational Change Amongst Ethnic Groups in Great Britain', (1992) 19 *New Community* 7.

8. The official statistics relating to this area distinguish between data relating to 'households' and that relating to 'families'. The notion of 'the household' covers 'a person living alone or a group of people living together'. By contrast, a 'family' encompasses 'a married, or cohabiting, couple with or without children, or a one parent with children'. People living alone are not considered to constitute a 'family'. *See*, for example, *Social Trends 24*, (HMSO London 1994), p. 35. Even taking a starting point free of such categorisations imposed by the official statistical series, however, an approach as apparently simplistic as considering notions of the 'nuclear family' as compared with the 'extended family' as a model for looking at this question is rendered highly complicated in the United Kingdom when regard is had to the considerable ethnic and cultural diversity of the modern resident population.

9. A significant change in the law relating to the grounds upon which divorce could be granted was introduced by the Divorce Reform Act of 1969, which came into force in 1971.

10. *1992 General Household Survey* (Office or Population Censuses and Surveys, Series GHS No. 23, HMSO London 1994), p. 7–8, and Table 2.23.

Table 1. Divorce: By duration of marriage (United Kingdom, percentages and 000s)

	Year of divorce			
Duration of marriage (percentages)	1961	1971	1981	1991
0–2 years	1.2	1.2	1.5	9.3
3–4 years	10.1	12.2	19.0	14.0
5–9 years	30.6	30.5	29.1	27.0
10–14 years	22.9	19.4	19.6	18.3
15–19 years	13.9	{ 12.6	12.8	12.8
20–24 years		{ 9.5	8.6	9.5
25–29 years	21.2	{ 5.8	4.9	5.0
30 years and over		{ 8.9	4.5	4.1
All durations (in 000s)	**27.0**	**79.2**	**155.6**	**171.1 (= 100%)**

Source: Social Trends 4 (HMSO London 1994), p. 38, Table 2.13.

than doubling of the rate for families with dependent children since 1971.[11]

Table 2. People in households: (by type of household and family in which they live) (Great Britain, percentages and 000s)

	1961	1971	1981	1991	1992
Living alone	3.9	6.3	8.0	10.7	11.1
Married couple, no children	17.8	19.3	19.5	23.0	23.4
Married couple with dependent children	52.2	51.7	47.4	41.1	39.9
Married couples with non-dependent children only	11.6	10.0	10.3	10.8	10.9
Lone parent with dependent children	2.5	3.5	5.8	10.0	10.1
Other households	12.0	9.2	9.0	4.3	4.6
All people in private households	**49,545**	**52,347**	**52,760**	**54,056**	...

Source: Social Trends 4 (HMSO London 1994), p. 35, Table 2.6.

When one looks at the overall make-up of households in Great Britain (Table 2), the pattern over the past thirty years can clearly be seen as one in which the 'normal pattern' of a married couple with dependent children has declined, while the proportion of people living alone, living as a married couple but without children, or living as lone parents with dependent children has risen markedly.

The important question in relation to the picture outlined hitherto is, therefore, how far it accords with any assumptions which serve to inform those who would seek to develop social policy for the United Kingdom. Here, the recent thrust of research in the social sciences – particularly in relation to patterns of kin support – indicates that something of a gap has developed between the 'model' assumed by

11. *Social Trends 24*, p. 36. Around a fifth of the lone parents in Great Britain in 1991 were aged under 25. Characteristics of lone-parent families include a greater likelihood to be living in local authority (public sector) accommodation; a lower level of qualifications; and a lower likelihood that the parent would be working. Such families also constitute a high proportion of those family units which are at the very lowest levels of income scales. (1992 *General Household Survey*, p. 8 and Tables 2.26 – 2.30). It may be noted, however, that these and the foregoing official statistics do not address the situation of 'stable' couples with children where the parents are not married – with the result that such social units do not appear in the statistical profiles for 'families' in the United Kingdom.

the policy-makers and the developments of the past quarter of a century.[12]

In particular, it has been suggested that a model of what has been labelled the 'gendered modified extended family' best serves the current picture,[13] according to which it is assumed that 'social policy is informed by a model . . . in which independent nuclear households, composed of a male breadwinner and his female dependent plus their immature children if they have any, are linked in a state of partial dependence upon each other'.[14]

Certainly, if this model provides anything like a realistic picture of the British case, any continuing assumption of 'the male breadwinner' – which appears to be capable of demonstrating remarkable longevity in the minds of policy makers and commentators alike – is something of a tribute to the gulf between aspiration and reality when it comes to integrating women into the workforce and providing them with equal opportunities for developing careers and 'breadwinning' capacity.

In any event, it is suggested that the picture conjured up by any model such as that of the 'gendered modified extended family' probably serves to confirm the extent of developments since the Beveridge Report stimulated one commentator to observe, in 1945, that:

> 'One of the happiest innovations proposed in the Beveridge Report is the emergence of the housewife as a separate and honoured category of the population. In wartime no one disputed the complete partnership of women in communal life and there is unstinted appreciation of her contribution to war industry. But rearing babies through happy, healthy childhood to independent maturity is even more important than wiring aeroplanes, and is a very much more absorbing and exacting task.'[15]

Even leaving aside the question of the 'political correctness' of such an observation in the context of today's debates in this area, and while it remains true that female rates of pay continue to lag behind those of males in the British labour market,[16] levels of female participation in the workforce have, as can be seen from Table 3 (which presents only the figures for persons in 'employee status' employment), been steadily rising, and the acceptance of 'the working wife' as well as the phenomenon of 'the working woman' as a normal state of affairs is, by now, firmly established throughout the great majority of British society.[17]

---

12. *See*, for example, J. Finch, *Family Obligations and Social Change* (Polity, Cambridge 1989), p. 124ff.
13. id.
14. *ibid.*, at p. 125. The notion that family life consists of 'a coalition of nuclear families in a state of partial dependence' is drawn from E. Litwak, 'Extended kin relations in a democratic industrial society', in E. Shanas & G. Streib (eds.), *Social Structure and the Family: Generational Relations* (Prentice Hall, New York 1965), at p. 291.
15. Gertrude Williams, in *Women and Work* (Nicholson & Watson, London 1945), cited in the 'Editor's Introduction' to R.E. Pahl (ed.), *On Work. Historical, Comparative & Theoretical Approaches* (Blackwell, Oxford 1988), p. 14.
16. Female employees working full-time one adult rates received 79% of the average hourly earnings of their male equivalents in 1992. For manual workers, the figure was 71% and for non-manual workers it was 67%. *See Women & Men in Britain 1993* (EOC, HMSO Manchester 1993), p. 19 and Tables 10.1 – 10.4.
17. Whether one is able to go so far as to claim that women have equal access to 'power' in career and general working terms is, however, a different issue. Certainly, the phenomenon of the 'glass ceiling' seems to be widely accepted as a real problem for women's careers in many parts of the United Kingdom labour market, although the evidence for this remains, naturally, largely anecdotal.

Table 3. Workforce Participation (Male and Female employees)[18]
(United Kingdom, in 000s, adjusted for seasonal variation)

		Employees in employment			
		Male		Female	
		All	*Part-time*	*All*	*Part-time*
1990					
	June	12,046		10,872	
	September	12,043		10,829	
	December	11,884		10,891	
1991					
	March	11,642		10,727	
	June	11,530		10,731	
	September	11,447	1,015	10,664	4,739
	December	11,343		10,709	
1992					
	March	11,228		10,675	
	June	11,211		10,695	
	September	11,042		10,508	
	December	10,969	1,140	10,585	4,830
1993					
	March	10,903	1,107	10,528	4,788
	June	10,928	1,121	10,626	4,851
	September	10,950	1,136	10,633	4,840
	December	10,881	1,156	10,695	4,947
1994					
	March	10,791	1,140	10,587	4,881

Source: (1994) *Employment Gazette* S6 (July 1994), Table 1.1.

Table 4. Economic activity rates: by sex, EC comparison, 1991

	Males	Females	All
Denmark	74.8	62.0	68.3
United Kingdom	75.0	53.0	63.6
Portugal	73.7	50.5	61.3
Germany	72.8	48.6	60.1
Netherlands	71.7	45.1	58.2
France	65.9	47.6	56.3
Irish Republic	72.6	37.0	54.6
Luxembourg	69.5	36.3	52.4
Italy	67.8	36.5	51.5
Belgium	62.4	38.5	50.0
Spain	66.9	33.3	49.3
Greece	65.8	33.7	49.1

Source: Eurostat. Cited in *Social Trends 24*, p. 58, Table 4.7

Indeed, over recent years the British female economic activity rate has been one of the highest in the European Communities, as can be seen from Table 4. Nev-

18. Note that these figures exclude the self-employed, members of HM Forces, and those involved on work-related government training programmes.

Table 5. Average hours usually worked per week: by sex, EC comparison, 1991

	Males	Females	All
Portugal	42.5	38.5	40.8
Greece	40.7	37.8	39.7
Spain	40.7	37.3	39.6
Irish Republic	41.0	34.9	38.5
Luxembourg	40.3	34.9	38.4
Italy	39.6	35.3	38.0
France	39.9	34.8	37.6
United Kingdom	43.5	30.3	37.3
Germany	39.5	32.6	36.6
Belgium	38.1	31.8	35.6
Denmark	36.4	31.6	34.1
Netherlands	35.7	25.9	31.9

Source: Eurostat. Cited in *Social Trends 24*, p. 60, Table 4.14.

Table 6. Full and part-time employment: by sex (United Kingdom, in 000s)

	Males		Females	
	Full-time	Part-time	Full-time	Part-time
1984	13,240	570	5,422	4,343
1985	13,336	575	5,503	4,457
1986	13,430	647	5,662	4,566
1987	13,472	750	5,795	4,696
1988	13,881	801	6,069	4,808
1989	14,071	734	6,336	4,907
1990	14,109	789	6,479	4,928
1991	13,686	799	6,350	4,933
1992	13,141	885	6,244	5,081
1993	12,769	886	6,165	5,045

Source: *Social Trends 24*, p. 59, Table 4.12.

ertheless, as appears from Table 5, the average hours worked by females in the United Kingdom is well towards the bottom of the 'European league table'.[19]

What thus emerges is a picture of something around one half of the female British population being active on the labour market, but with the overwhelming

19. There is also a fierce debate over the question of whether female workers 'choose' part-time work in preference to other forms of employment, or whether the incidence of part-time work amongst the female workforce is a consequence of women having to accept the only realistic forms of work which are on offer to them. On the basis of data such as that *infra* at Table 9, a variety of British government publications have tended to promote a view that women prefer part-time working because of its perceived potential for personal flexibility, while the advantages to employers of part-time working patterns are regularly to be found under discussion – *e.g.* as by A. Evans & T. Attew, 'Alternatives to full time permanent staff', in C. Curson (ed), *Flexible Patterns of Work* (IPM, London 1986), at p. 102ff. – apparently on the same assumption that election to work part-time is a free choice exercised commonly by female members of the workforce. Little direct data for the United Kingdom appears to support either position on this point. However, the issue of such 'employment ideology' as a factor in presentations of labour market circumstances has been addressed for the Swedish case by A. Christensen, Lönearbetet som samhällsform och ideologi. Sociala värderingsförändringar (Delrapport från projektet värderingsförskjutningar i det svenska samhället, Sekretariatet för framtidsstudier, U.o., 1983). For comparative comment on this approach, *see* A. Neal, 'Vulnerable Workers in Sweden and Britain', in A. Neal & A. Victorin (eds), *Law and the Weaker Party, Volume V – The Comparison II* (Butterworths, London 1992), at p. 92ff.

majority of those female workers engaged in part-time work, compared with working males, amongst whom full-time employment remains the norm *(Table 6)*.

Table 7. Characteristics of households participating in the Family Expenditure Survey – Married women and dependent children

	Percentage of all households	Number of households
Households with married women economically active	**31.9**	**2,364**
With no dependant children	16.2	1,199
With dependant children	15.7	1,165
One child	5.7	423
Two children	7.5	560
Three children	1.9	143
Four or more children	0.5	39
Households with married women not economically active	**25**	**1,851**
With no dependant children	16.5	1,225
With dependant children	8.4	626
One child	2.7	203
Two children	3.4	252
Three children	1.4	102
Four or more children	0.9	69
Number of households surveyed with married women	**56.8**	**4,215**
Number of households surveyed without married women	**43.2**	**3,203**

Source: Family Spending. A report on the 1992 Family Expenditure Survey (CSO, HMSO London 1993), p. 2, Table 1.

Amongst that economically active female workforce, it is possible to obtain an indication of where the factor of dependent children enters the picture by looking at data from the 1992 Family Expenditure Survey (Table 7). Although this data only derives from a limited survey of just over 7,000 households and is limited to looking at situations where there is a married woman in those households, the indications appear to be that the modern British picture is increasingly one of households containing economically active women who seek to combine motherhood with a continuation of their active status on the labour market. Amongst the reasons put forward for this trend, in addition to the increased availability of part-time jobs in the economy, has been a recorded rise in the average age at which women have children[20] – although there have recently been signs of this rise in the rate of economic activity amongst younger women being off-set to some extent by an increase in the numbers of such women entering further and higher education.[21]

(II) Policies at the Legislative/Regulatory Level

It has been suggested that the development of modern social policy in the United Kingdom is informed by a 'model' – the so-called 'gendered modified extended fam-

20. The mean age of mothers at birth in England and Wales rose from 26.8 years in 1981 to 27.9 years in 1992. *See Social Trends 24*, (HMSO London 1994), p. 27, Table 1.12.
21. *Social Trends 24*, (HMSO London 1994), p. 57–58 and Table 3.10.

ily' – which makes certain assumptions about the make-up of family units and, consequently, about the relationships of such model family profiles to the labour market. By the same token, one can ask whether the implementation of social policy – particularly through legislative means – is also informed by a 'model' which proceeds from certain given assumptions.

In the course of presenting a comparison of the phenomenon of 'vulnerable workers' in Sweden and Britain, this author has suggested that it may be possible to identify a number of elements in British legislation which indicate the kinds of assumptions upon which the legislator operates in relation to labour law matters.[22] That presentation, which drew upon legislative and administrative provisions in force in the mid-1980s, indicated that the 'typology' for employment in Britain turns out broadly as follows:

> 'An 'employee' (as defined in statutory terms), between the ages of 18 and 60 (women) or 65 (men), who has worked in stable (in terms of hours worked and/or length of service) circumstances directly for the same employer on a permanent basis at that employer's workplace, without withdrawing from the labour market at any stage either voluntarily or involuntarily.'

It was also suggested that 'the profile (while in practice undoubtedly being substantially influenced) is ostensibly unaffected from the legislator's point of view by factors such as sex, marital status, race, ethnic origin, politics, trade union membership or payment system. It remains an open question, of course, as to how far factors such as these nevertheless operate differentially in practice'.[23]

During the eight years since that profile was put forward, there have been a number of quite radical changes to United Kingdom labour law legislation – a number of which impact directly upon the 'model profile', and suggest the need for modification of the 'typology' put forward for the mid-1980s.[24] In particular, the influence of regulations derived from the level of the European Communities has obliged the British legislator to respond with a range of positive law rights, enshrined in statutes or secondary legislation, in areas of labour law which it might have been thought would not otherwise have received such treatment.[25] These aspects of legislative activity include matters of health and safety at work and enhanced protection for

---

22. Alan C. Neal, 'Vulnerable Workers in Sweden and Britain', in A. Neal & A. Victorin, *Law and the Weaker Party, Volume V* (Butterworths, London 1992).
23. *ibid*, at p. 98.
24. *See*, for example, the equally pertinent observations of S. Fredman, 'European Community discrimination law: a critique', (1992) 21 *Industrial Law Journal* 119. More fundamental critique is to be found in work such as N. Lacey, 'Legislation Against Sex Discrimination: Questions from a Feminist Perspective', (1987) 14 *Journal of Law and Society* 114.
25. It is characteristic of United Kingdom implementation for Community legislation (particularly Directives) in the social field that this has been undertaken largely through direct prescriptive legislative means. This contrasts with a number of Member States of the European Union where such implementation is either done through 'framework' regulations or, sometimes, in conjunction with the social partners on the domestic labour market. The level of compliance with the European Community obligations in this field is extremely high, and is to be seen not only in relation to transposition of Directives (*see*, for example, *Ninth annual report to the European Parliament on Commission monitoring of the application of Community law – 1991* OJ/C 250/01, at 250/29, and, for the most recent report, 1994 OJ/C 154/35) but also when shortcomings in such transposition are brought to the attention of the government or the courts (*see*, for example, the observations of the European Court of Justice in Cases C-382/92 and C-383/92 *Commission v. United Kingdom*). *See* also the Commission's 1994 White Paper *European Social Policy: A Way Forward for the Union,* Chapter 10, Table 1.

women during pregnancy and for nursing mothers,[26] and will eventually include a limited measure of regulation for working hours.[27] There has also been increasing concern to ensure that part-time workers do not suffer discrimination where this could be seen as a form of 'indirect discrimination' against women.[28]

In the light of such changes – whether or not the British legislator can claim to have undertaken the change of heart willingly – therefore, it may be suggested that a modified 'typology' of worker informing the assumptions of the law-makers in the United Kingdom might be as follows:

> 'An 'employee' (as defined in statutory terms), between the ages of 18 and 65, who has worked in stable (in terms of hours worked and/or length of service) circumstances directly for the same employer on a permanent basis at that employer's workplace, without withdrawing from the labour market at any stage either voluntarily or involuntarily other than in relation to childbearing.'

While the current legislation continues to occupy a stance of 'formal neutrality' in relation to gender, marital status, race, ethnic origin, politics, trade union membership or payment system, it is arguable that, in some respects, the pendulum has shifted in the direction of offering specially enhanced protections for certain groups identified as particularly vulnerable in the labour market.[29] However, it is probably too early to judge whether this is irrevocably the case, and it suffices to note the relatively minor shift between the 'typology' presented for the mid-1980s and that suggested as holding good for the mid-1990s.

(III) Comment

In the foregoing it has been suggested that both social policy makers (at the political and governmental level) and social policy implementers (primarily, at the level of the legislator) operate in the United Kingdom on the basis of a variety of assumptions about family life and working life which are built into model profiles or 'typologies'. However, it is also suggested that the models used for each of those functions may not adequately reflect the picture of household and family units in Britain or the patterns of economic activity which have developed for the labour

---

26. For fuller treatment of the flood of measures developed in the wake of the 'framework' Directive 89/391/EEC in the field of health and safety at work, *see* Alan C. Neal, 'The European Framework Directive on the Health and Safety of Workers: Challenges for the United Kingdom?', (1990) 6 *International Journal of Comparative Labour Law and Industrial Relations* 80, together with A. Neal & F. Wright, *The European Communities' Health and Safety Legislation* (Chapman & Hall, London 1992). Changes prompted by Directive 92/85/EEC on the introduction of measures to encourage improvements in the safety and health at work of pregnant workers and workers who have recently given birth or are breastfeeding will take effect on 14 October 1994, through the bringing into force of provisions in the Trade Union Reform and Employment Rights Act 1993 and the Management of Health and Safety (Amendment) Regulations 1994.
27. However, Directive 93/104/EC, of 23 November 1993, concerning certain aspects of the organisation of working time, is currently the subject of a challenge by the United Kingdom government before the European Court of Justice. *See* (1994) *Employment Gazette* 106 (April 1994), reporting an answer to a Parliamentary question given on 16 March 1994.
28. *See*, most dramatically, the recent Opinion of the House of Lords in the case of *R.* v. *Secretary of State for Employment, ex parte Equal Opportunities Commission and another* [1994] 2 W.L.R. 409, for comment in relation to which see, too, M. Ross, 'The British EOC Case – A Model of Compliance?', (1994) 10 *The International Journal of Comparative Labour Law and Industrial Relations* 139.
29. *See* Alan C. Neal, 'O Brave New World', (1994) 144 *New Law Journal* 1070.

market. With a view to indicating some of the outstanding problems in relation to the combining, overlapping or integration of working life with family life in Britain, therefore, a few words will be said about issues arising in three key fields: (i) arrangements for childcare; (ii) arrangements for working parents with older children; and (iii) arrangements for addressing the problems of a relatively ageing British population. Each of these situations presents a challenge at the interface of working life and family life.

THE INTERFACE BETWEEN WORKING LIFE AND FAMILY LIFE

(I) Children and Childcare

It is perhaps in relation to the problem posed for working mothers of caring for their children during working time that the most effective stimulus to the debate on the relationship between family life and working life has been provided.

This comes as little surprise, given the participation rates for younger women (Table 4) and the proportion of households containing both economically active married women and dependent children (Table 7). However, what comes as more of a surprise is the remarkable reticence on the part of the State to make provision for childcare facilities in order to ameliorate some of the more problematic organisational aspects of 'juggling work and home'. This is of particular concern for working mothers, who, it has been suggested, are still assumed to – and, in practice, do – take on the bulk of this responsibility, whether in terms of feeding and supervising children, transporting them to and from school or nursery, or providing the 'domestic infra-structure' of cleaning, washing, shopping, and the myriad other tasks arising in any household.[30]

Table 8. Proportion of families with children under five using facilities for childcare: by mother's economic activity status, 1991 (Great Britain (percentages))

	Mother's economic activity status				
	Working full-time	Working part-time	Unemployed	Economically inactive	All mothers
School/nursery school	29	35	19	19	25
Unpaid family or friends	36	38	19	15	24
Private or voluntary scheme	11	20	16	17	17
Paid child minder/nanny	38	15	3	2	11
Local authority scheme	3	7	5	8	7
Workplace facility	3	1	...	...	1
Any childcare facility	81	82	53	51	64

Source: General Household Survey. Cited in *Social Trends* 24 (1994 edition, HMSO), p. 36, Table 2.10.

30. *See* generally on this, J.Finch, *Family Obligations and Social Change* (Polity, Cambridge 1989). Similar assumptions are indicated in B.Jordan, M.Redley & S.James, *Putting the Family First* (UCL Press, London 1994), and in several of the contributions contained in S.Arber & N.Gilbert (eds.), *Women and Working Lives: Divisions and Change* (British Sociological Association, Macmillan, Basingstoke 1992), as well as in the rather more polemical contributions in C.Curson (ed.), *Flexible Patterns of Work* (IPM, London 1986).

Indeed, it may be suggested that the United Kingdom suffers from remarkably poor public sector provision of child-minding and childcare (crêches, nursery schools, etc.) facilities, and that this fact, coupled with insignificant tax incentives for private sector employers to provide workplace childcare facilities,[31] is responsible for a pattern of provision which relies primarily upon school supervision or the unpaid support of family or friends (Table 8).

(II) Working Parents

The continuing need to provide care for dependent children in the absence of significant State or employer provision is only one of several factors which have given impetus to the debate over 'flexible work forms' from the point of view of organisation of working time and hours.[32] From that 'flexibility' debate have been spawned a variety of issues, including renewed concentration upon the patterns of working hours commonly worked in British enterprises, as well as more 'visionary' discussion of phenomena variously described as 'homeworking', 'networking', and other exploitation of (in particular) information technology to enable workers to perform their work tasks from home.

One of the most important tasks, therefore, has been to discover what kinds of work regimes are regarded by workers as being either convenient or inconvenient – an issue over which it would appear that there are sharply diverging views as between men and women (Table 9).

The extent to which so-called 'unsocial hours' work regimes are rejected by both full-time and part-time working women as compared with their male counterparts stands out as a particular point of note, particularly when one considers that the traditional notion of 'unsocial hours' coincides largely with the kinds of family lifestyles normally regarded as necessary for bringing up and caring for dependent children.

Another sharp contrast can be seen between the genders when comparison is made of the reasons for unemployed persons having left their last job. Here, the

---

31. Indeed, until very recently, there was almost no way of setting the costs of childcare against personal tax liability, and, even now – and in spite of some much heralded initiatives by a number of large employers, notably in the financial services sector (most of which appear very quickly to have been discontinued or scaled-down – what possibility there might be provides little in the way of encouragement for an improvement of the situation.
32. The debate over the so-called 'flexible firm' has concentrated largely upon 'internal flexibility' of the firm – often by reference to notions such as 'numerical flexibility' or 'functional flexibility'. *See*, for example, J. Atkinson, *Manning for Uncertainty: Some emerging UK Work Patterns* (University of Sussex Institute of Manpower Studies, Brighton 1984), and J. Atkinson, 'Manpower strategies for flexible organisations', (1984) *Personnel Management* 28. The terminology has passed into common usage, although the model of 'the flexible firm' has given rise to criticism: *see*, for example, A. Pollert, 'The flexible firm: fixation or fact?', (1988) 2 *Work, Employment and Society* 281, and, for a robust rejection of the Pollert view, C. Hakim, 'Workforce Re-structuring in Europe in the 1980s', (1989) 5 *International Journal of Comparative Labour Law and Industrial Relations* 167, at pp. 170–172. Only relatively recently have issues concerning what might be termed 'external flexibility' received similarly widespread attention. Mention needs also to be made of the formal introduction of equal opportunities policies and laws – notwithstanding the cynicism sometimes directed towards such developments (as indicated *supra* at note 5) – particularly through responses to initiatives at the European Communities level. *See*, in particular, the United Kingdom responses mentioned *supra* at note 4, together with the particular concentration in the case law of the European Court of Justice upon employment related benefits and career development issues within the context of equal opportunities and equal pay provisions.

Table 9. Extent to which various work regimes are perceived as inconvenient (percentages)

	Men	Women Full-time	Women Part-time	All
Work full-time standard	4	10	50	18
Work 1 hour later	7	18	19	13
Work Saturdays	15	34	41	26
Start before 8 am	10	37	63	30
Work after 6 pm	16	40	50	31
Work Sundays	30	51	60	43
Work early/late shifts	35	52	69	48
Be away overnight regularly	43	67	82	59
Work split shifts	54	67	74	62
Work after 11 pm	53	80	80	66
Work rotating shifts	54	73	85	67
Work overnight	55	81	83	68
(Average N)	*(710)*	*(320)*	*(372)*	*(1,403)*

Source: Catherine Marsh, *Hours of Work of Women and Men in Britain* (EOC Research Series, HMSO London, 1991), p. 76, Table 10.4.

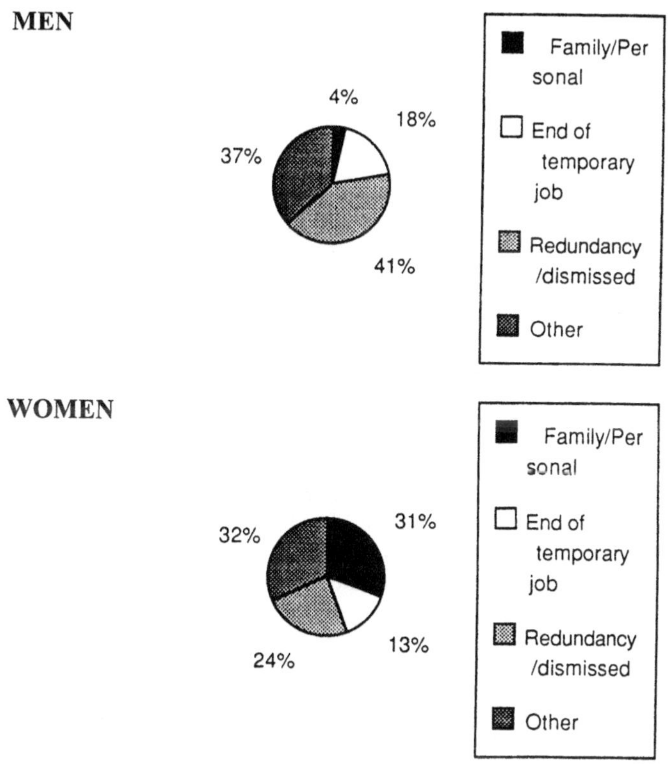

Figure 1. Unemployed (ILO defined): reason for leaving last job (Great Britain: Spring 1993)

Source: Labour Force Survey estimates. Cited in (1994) *Employment Gazette* 252 (July 1994).

proportion of men citing 'family or personal reasons' for having left their last employment is put at only some 4%, whereas 31% of women gave this as their primary reason (Figure 1). Once again, these indications serve to support the proposition that it is still primarily women, even though they may be seeking to remain economically active, who, when the need arises, are called upon to provide family care and support other than through the economic 'breadwinning' role.[33]

Table 10. People working at home in main job by industry and occupation (Great Britain, Autumn 1993, figures in 000s)

	All	Men	Women
Paid employees and self-employed working in own home	**662**	**195**	**466**
Industry:			
Manufacturing	97	23	74
Non-manufacturing	564	172	390
Occupation:			
Managers & administrators	151	64	86
Professional	70	40	30
Associate professional & technical	105	49	56
Clerical & secretarial	147	5	142
Craft & related	49	15	33
Plant & machine operatives	16	2	14
Other	124	20	104
Who they work for:			
for an outside organisation	113	32	80
on their own account	346	126	219
for a family business	203	37	165
Others working in own home or using home as a base			
Unpaid family workers working in their own home	65	15	50
People doing paid work in different places with home as a base	1,581	1,268	316

Source: Labour Force Survey. Cited in (1994) *Employment Gazette* LFS4 (June 1994).

However, any suggestion that the perceived requirement for 'flexibility' is being met through new forms of work enabling those with family responsibilities to remain physically at home while still performing their work tasks remains open to serious doubt, as emerges from Table 10. The low numbers of workers encompassed by such regimes in 1993 – a total of only some 662,000 throughout Great Britain – would appear to give the lie to 'bullish' journalistic accounts of the rapid spread of such arrangements, while the preponderance of self-employed persons or those working for a family business suggests that no major impact has yet been made by the availability of enhanced computing and telecommunications facilities.[34]Indeed, there seems little reason to imagine that any dramatic change on this front is to be

33. A separate, although related, phenomenon tending to underline this position can be seen in respect of statistics measuring the incidence of withdrawal of 'second earners' from labour market activity when the 'main earner' suffers unemployment. *See*, for example, G. Leighton, 'Wives' and Husbands', Labour Market Participation and Household Resource Distribution in the Context of Middle-class Male Unemployment', in S. Arber & N. Gilbert (eds), *Women and Working Lives: Divisions and Change* (MacMillan, Basingstoke 1992), Chapter 9.

34. *See*, for example, the observation quoted in Alan C. Neal, 'Atypical Workforms and European Labour Law', (1989) 45 *Recht der Arbeit* 115, at p. 115, footnote 7.

expected in the short-term, while, as far as the longer term is concerned, doubts being raised about the absence of 'social intercourse' with colleagues at the workplace and associated feelings of isolation on the parts of homeworkers may prove more of a brake upon widespread developments of this kind than had perhaps been imagined.[35]

Overall, therefore, there is relatively little in the way of practical provision in the United Kingdom to achieve 'external flexibility' in working life of a kind which could more easily allow the discharge of family responsibilities. In particular, apart from statutory arrangements to facilitate maternity leave for expectant mothers and ancillary time off work,[36] there has been no significant development of mechanisms such as sabbaticals, extended leave, or 'career breaks',[37] while proposals at the level of the European Union to introduce statutory entitlements to 'Paternity Leave' have met with a distinctly hostile reception from the present British government.

(III) Caring for an Ageing Population

Table 11. Age and sex structure of the United Kingdom population (percentages and millions)

	%					(millions)
	Under 16	16–39	40–64	65–79	80 and over	All ages
Mid-year estimates						
1961	24.9	31.4	32.0	9.8	1.9	**52.8**
1971	25.5	31.3	29.9	10.9	2.3	**55.9**
1981	22.3	34.9	27.8	12.2	2.8	**56.4**
1991	20.3	35.3	28.6	12.0	3.7	**57.8**
Males	21.4	36.7	29.0	10.6	2.3	**28.2**
Females	19.3	34.0	28.2	13.3	5.2	**29.6**
Mid-year projections						
2001	21.0	32.8	30.5	11.4	4.2	**59.7**
2011	19.5	30.3	33.7	11.9	4.7	**61.1**
2021	18.5	30.0	32.3	14.0	5.2	**62.0**
2031	18.4	28.7	30.3	15.6	6.9	**62.1**
Males	19.0	29.7	30.9	14.9	5.5	**30.7**
Females	17.7	27.8	29.8	16.4	8.3	**31.4**

Source: Social Trends 24 (1994 edition, HMSO), p. 23, Table 1.4

A third aspect of the interface between 'family life' and 'working life' arises in relation to the care of the elderly. The United Kingdom, in common with most

35. It is suggested that great caution needs to be exercised when considering accounts of 'homeworking' or 'networking' such as those presented in C. Curson (ed.), *Flexible Patterns of Work* (IPM, London 1986), especially at p. 128ff.

36. Contained in the Employment Protection (Consolidation) Act 1978, as amended by the Trade Union Reform and Employment Rights Act 1993. A substantially overhauled framework for these rights takes effect from 14th October 1994 – largely in response to obligations deriving from the level of the European Union.

37. Indeed, these tend to be regarded in management eyes as either some form of 'reward for good service', as a response to some urgent crisis in the home, or as something connected directed with professional training or education. Relatively little provision appears to exist, for example, to complement statutory maternity leave provisions in order to allow for substantial periods (in the order of, say, five years) of absence from work – and, where these do exist, the general pattern would appear to be based on there being no pay during any such period. *See*, in relation to the limited British experience, A. Evans & P. Massey, 'Sabbaticals, extended leave and career breaks', in C. Curson (ed.), *Flexible Patterns of Work* (IPM, London 1986), especially at p. 166ff.

Western European nations, has an ageing population,[38] with all of the pressures which this brings in terms of social care provision. Furthermore, as emerges from Table 11, this trend is projected to continue, so that it is expected that the dependent population (the combined number of children and pensioners) for every 100 people of working age[39] will have risen from a 1951 figure of 57, through a level of 63 by 1991, to a level of 79 by the year 2031.[40]

Commentators concerned with kin relationships in British society have looked, in particular, at relationships of parent–child support, and have suggested that, where this is in the direction of care for the aged parent, there exists a strong need for a balance to be struck between dependence upon the child and an appropriate degree of personal independence for the aged parent.[41]

Such researchers have also pointed to another important dimension of such caring relationships – namely, gender. Thus, it is suggested that 'there is evidence that men, even where they acknowledge that they have responsibilities to parents ... often exercise those responsibilities through their wives. Sons commonly provide personal care and practical support for their elderly parents through the use of their wives' labour rather than their own'.[42]

The picture, once again, therefore, indicates that the 'default' burden of caring for ageing parents is most likely to fall upon a female child, thereby placing still further pressures upon any attempt on the parts of such women to maintain active participation in the labour market along with the discharge of family responsibilities.

Here, too, recent British government policies in relation to withdrawal of State provision of care for the elderly appear to assume, under the banner of 'family values', that the willingness and the ability to care for the ageing population is to be found in the increasingly 'normal' family units with economically active female members – an assumption which, far from cementing family ties in some idealised 'Victorian extended family' sense, may turn out to contain the seeds of such severe tensions between dependent kin that a withdrawal of 'traditional' family caring patterns might accompany the already witnessed withdrawal of State care for the elderly.[43]

(IV) Comment

The broad conclusion to be drawn from these (limited) glimpses of problems at the interface of family life and working life is that, in terms of provision to ease the burden of caring for children, the United Kingdom does little apart from the granting of statu-

38. *See Social Trends 24*, (HMSO London 1994), p. 21 and Table 1.5.
39. What is described as 'the dependency ratio'.
40. *Social Trends 24*, (HMSO London 1994), p. 23.
41. *See*, for example, J. Finch, *Family Obligations and Social Change* (Polity, Cambridge 1989), at p. 36ff.
42. J.Finch, *Family Obligations and Social Change* (Polity, Cambridge 1989), at p. 40 – an observation which leads, in part, to the author's conclusion that '... much of the empirical evidence on parent–child support betrays a sense of wariness and carefulness about offering and accepting such support, which is far removed from the idea that it is the most natural thing in the world for parents and children to support each other' (*ibid*, at p. 41).
43. It may be, too, that similar trends towards the replacement of State welfare provision by assumed care provision from family relatives in the context of health care for the sick and disabled – promoted under the political slogan of 'Care in the Community' – would give rise to similar tensions for the presumptive carers.

tory entitlements to paid time off work for expectant and new mothers. Nor is there any substantial evidence of a new 'flexibility' being made available in relation to the organisation of work and working time in order to reduce the conflicts between (for example) school timetables and the normal patterns of British working regimes. The same absence of any new flexibility impacts upon the ability to combine working life with care of elderly relatives, and, coupled with government policies to encourage 'private' rather than 'State' provision in this respect, suggests that additional tensions are being created by virtue of the ageing population of the United Kingdom.

In the majority of cases, both the widely accepted societal 'role models' and the reality point towards a continuation of the 'twin burden' being particularly felt by parent members of the female workforce.

OVERVIEW OF THE UNITED KINGDOM PICTURE

The debate surrounding 'family life' and 'working life' is well developed and has presently taken on a particular significance in terms of social policy generation for the United Kingdom in the 1990s. That debate has been taking place against a background which has, to some extent, moved away from the 'Beveridge model' of the modern Welfare State based upon social insurance. Instead, since 1979, there has been a shift towards a more *laissez-faire* attitude towards individual responsibilities within society and a withdrawal (notably in terms of financial provision for social security) of the State from a range of care provision which had previously been taken for granted as falling within the ambit of the responsibilities of the State.

At the same time, however, demographic change and marked changes in attitude towards 'traditional values' touching upon family life – coupled, it is claimed, with some of the direct consequences of the new 'hands off' approach adopted by the State – have brought about a very different pattern of social relations and working patterns from those recognised as the norm for the United Kingdom only a quarter of a century ago. In the context of 'family life', the increase in lone-parent family units, the emergence of 'dual breadwinners' within more 'traditional' family units, and the need to have regard to an increasingly ageing population are worthy of mention. As regards 'working life', the widespread availability of part-time work, increasing levels of female economic activity, and pressures towards a more 'flexible' framework for work are of particular note – especially when considering responsibilities for the care and upbringing of children.

In spite of dramatic changes which are under way, however, it appears that the underlying assumptions for both social policy makers and for those charged with the task of implementing social policy are of a more 'traditional' kind – the 'gendered modified extended family' and the legislator's 'typology' of stable long-term employment with a single employer. This disparity, it is suggested, is further heightened by the political rhetoric of 'family values', which itself appears to hark back to some 'golden era' and to embody individual responsibilities and caring patterns without the need for anything more than a 'minimum safety net' of State insurance or assistance.

It has also to be recalled that the United Kingdom is not a society regulated by principles contained in a written Constitution, nor has the traditional pattern of protective social legislation established mechanisms such as minimum wage levels or statutory regulation of working time. Nevertheless, influences at the international level are now clearly bringing about a change in this latter phenomenon of 'legal abstentionism', particularly through the wide range of positive law rights derived from Directives enacted by the European Union. Whether or not this influence meets with the approval of the United Kingdom's political masters may, however, be questioned, although there is no doubt that, once an international obligation of this kind has been assumed, there is a high level of loyalty shown towards discharge of that obligation. One may, therefore, be fairly confident in anticipating that, now that the legislative instrument has established itself firmly as the predominant mechanism for effecting social policy (and, in particular, labour market policy), one significant element in any future response to the perceived problems posed at the interface of working life and family life will be an extension of the body of statutory rules.

In summary, therefore, the United Kingdom case would appear to suggest that, while political rhetoric recognises the need for social policies directed towards the harmonisation of working life and family life, in reality there is a gap between those expressed political aspirations and the current situation both in respect of family policy and labour market policy. Much of that gap is attributable to unrealistic 'models' or assumptions informing those involved in social policy making and implementation.

While the 'value' of involving and integrating female workers into the labour market has long been accepted, the current instruments ostensibly designed to promote this objective would appear not to be adequately achieving that goal. Such 'equal opportunities' measures as do exist have been largely on the level of legislative provisions,[44] and it is suggested that the function of such measures may be undermined by an absence of supportive frameworks and mechanisms across a range of 'non-legal' arrangements in modern British society.

Meanwhile, the challenge of an ageing population has been met with a variety of government policies (many of which do not obviously form part of 'traditional labour law') which proceed on highly optimistic assumptions about the willingness, or the ability, of families to care for the elderly, the sick, and the infirm. Far from establishing the foundations for new patterns of kin care and support, there is a danger that the additional economic and moral pressures to which such policies give rise may serve to undermine the already existing patterns of care and support between relatives which continue to be found in many areas of modern British society.

The effective harmonisation of 'working life' and 'family life' in the United Kingdom has undoubtedly not been achieved to date. Unfortunately, it would also appear that such policies as are in place for addressing this problem may not only be inappropriate to changing circumstances – or, indeed, for the purpose of achieving some measure of harmonisation at all – but may actually be serving to heighten the problems in this sensitive area. So far, at least, it has to be said that the ideology of 'the market' and an ideal of 'family values' drawn from some supposedly former 'Golden Era' are proving to be poor substitutes for post-war social provision within the framework of the 'Welfare State'.

---

44. Although examples are to be found of some public sector promotion through the mechanism of so-called 'contract compliance' measures.

United States of America

Janice R. Bellace

1. INTRODUCTION

A review of the pattern of increasing female labor force participation in the United States over the last twenty-five years and of the development of policies designed to harmonize working and family life reveals two striking facts. First, there has been a substantial time lag between the increase in the labor force participation rate of women with young children and the development of any policies seeking to permit women to harmonize their work and family obligations. Second, the development of 'pro-family' policies has occurred mostly as the result of voluntary efforts by private sector businesses. Compared to other countries, the government has not been a leader in mandating or strongly encouraging child care leaves, nor has it established child care centers.

2. CHILDBEARING AND CHILD CARE NEEDS

2.1. Sex Discrimination Law

The first, major federal anti-discrimination statute was enacted in 1964. The Civil Rights Act is a broad-ranging statute, with Title VII covering discrimination in employment. When the Civil Rights Act was drafted, its main focus was discrimination against black persons. A prohibition against sex was not included until the bill was being debated on the floor of Congress. As a result, there was a paucity of legislative history to assist the courts in interpreting what Congress meant by the ban on sex discrimination. Moreover, the media coverage of Title VII focused on race discrimination. The newly-established Equal Employment Opportunity Commission (EEOC) issued its first guidelines on sex discrimination in 1965. The EEOC did not deem unlawful various employer practices, particularly with regard to pregnant women, that today would be unlawful. In general, the 1965 guidelines were rather mild.

Cases alleging sex discrimination began filtering into the federal appellate courts around 1970. The courts tended to take a strict view of the statute. If an employer had a different policy for women than it had for women, the courts deemed the policy unlawful. In some cases, employers argued that their differential treatment of women was required by state law. For instance, a state law might forbid women from lifting weights over thirty pounds, or might prohibit women in factories from working night work. The lower federal courts confronted by this argument unanimously struck down state protective laws as inconsistent with Title VII, a federal statute which was viewed as displacing contrary state law.[1]

The first sex discrimination case to reach the United States Supreme Court did so before the Supreme Court fully developed the conceptual apparatus for analyzing discrimination cases.[2] In *Phillips v. Martin Marietta Corporation*,[3] the company had a policy at its Georgia plant of not accepting job applications from women with pre-school aged children. The company did accept job applications from men with pre-school aged children. The company admitted overt differential treatment based on sex, but argued that it did not discriminate against women. The company noted that it did hire women, it simply did not hire women with young children because of these employees' greater absenteeism rate. The Supreme Court held unanimously that Martin Marietta had violated Title VII. The Court noted that the company had refused to hire every woman with pre-school aged children, thus discriminating against a whole category of persons regardless of an individual woman's ability to arrange for child care that would permit her to be a reliable employee.

The 1971 *Phillips* case had an immediate impact. Companies were compelled to review their employment policies so as to eliminate those that on their face discriminated on the basis of sex. In the same period, Congress was reviewing Title VII in response to criticism that its remedies and the powers of the EEOC were too weak. The 1972 amendments to Title VII significantly strengthened the statute's remedies and the powers of the EEOC. In 1972, the EEOC issues new guidelines on sex discrimination. The 1972 guidelines reflect the EEOC's greater understanding of what constitutes sex discrimination. Specific guidelines not only enlarged upon the 1965 interpretation, some also completely reversed the 1965 view. This occurred particularly with regard to the treatment of pregnant employees and new mothers.

2.1.1. Pregnancy and Maternity

The specific issue which was to reach the Supreme Court concerned whether an employer's disability and medical insurance plan[4] could exclude coverage for disabilities arising from pregnancy or childbirth. The 1965 guidelines had taken the view that it was lawful under Title VII for an employer to exclude such coverage. In its 1972 guidelines, the EEOC reversed its position. Many large companies refused to comply with the new guideline. In 1976, the Supreme Court, in *General Electric Company v. Gilbert*,[5] held that exclusion of pregnancy and childbirth from the coverage of an employer health insurance plan did not violate Title VII. The reasoning of the majority was grounded on the fact that the coverage offered male and female employees was identical, and that Title VII does not require an employer to cover-

---

1. Thus, the courts did not have to confront the issue squarely presented in most other countries; namely, that the same legislature which enacted the protective legislation subsequently enacted a sex equality statute but made no statement about the continuing validity of the protective legislation. In the United States, the federal courts could state that Congress had a a certain legislative objective and that inconsistent state legislation had to fall before the federal legislative objective.
2. By the mid-1970s, cases were deemed disparate treatment or disparate impact cases. The Phillips case was a disparate treatment case, but the Supreme Court in considering the defendant employer's argument veered towards a disparate impact analysis.
3. 400 U.S. 542 (1971).
4. Here it should be noted that the United States does not have a national health system or a national medical insurance system. Most persons receive health insurance through their own or a family member's coverage under an employer's plan.
5. 429 U.S. 125 (1976).

age additional risks unique to women. Suffice it to say that the case illustrates the limited reach of a concept of sexual equality that uses the standard of what is offered men as the statutory guarantee of what must be offered females.

The Supreme Court's decision in *Gilbert* generated a storm of protest. In an astonishingly short period of time, Congress reversed the impact of the decision in the Pregnancy Discrimination Act of 1978 (PDA). There were three problems with this statute. First, it had an extremely narrow focus. It was directed mostly at employee benefit plan coverage. It did nothing for those employees without health insurance coverage. Second, it refused to treat pregnancy as a unique condition. Rather, it treated pregnancy as a disability and said that employers should treat pregnant women the same as they would treat other employees similarly affected in their ability to work. As a result, a pregnant woman who felt she had been treatly unlawfully had to determine how the same employer had treated a non-pregnant person who was similarly affected in his or her ability to work. In most instances, no comparable non-pregnant person could be found. Third, the Pregnancy Discrimination Act completely ignored what occurs once the baby is born. The PDA was not designed to be maternity leave legislation.

By 1977, the main outlines of statutory law were already set. There have been no significant amendments of Title VII since then, with the exception of 1992 amendments that relate mostly to issues of proof. It was not until 1993 that Congress would enact legislation that would address the issue of maternity leave.

2.2. Increasing Female Labor Force Participation

Despite the lack of legislation supporting maternity and child care leave and the paucity of child care centers, the percentage of American women in the labor force rose steadily throughout the 1970s and 1980s. This phenomenon might not have happened without two other key events. First, the availability of reliable methods of contraception, especially the birth control pill, occurred at the beginning of the 1970s. This ability to prevent pregnancy, to time pregnancies, and to limit family size, undoubtedly contributed to the ability of younger women to remain attached to the labor force. Second, economic necessity (arising from the oil crises of the 1970s and the resultant recession) compelled many married women with young children to remain attached to the labor force. This latter fact is important. Historically, poorer women, unmarried women and those women without the support of a husband have worked in much larger numbers than married women with a husband present. Yet, a majority of females age 25–44 are married with children, and most of these have a husband present. Thus, female labor force participation rates would not have risen substantially unless married women with children went out to work.[6]

The increase in the numbers of married women with children who work has been the most dramatic[7] In 1970, 51.3% of all married mothers with children under 18 worked at some time during the year. In 1992, 72.9% did. Equally striking is the

---

6. At the present time there are approximately 57.6 million women in the labor force. About 30% of these are married mothers, and their families constitute about 25% of the total 68.8 million American families. Unmarried mothers make up about 10% of the female labor force participants, and their families constitute about 8% of all families.
7. The data cited on this topic is reported in Howard V. Hayghe and Suzanne M. Bianchi, 'Married mothers' work patterns: the job-family compromise', *Monthly Labor Review*, Vol. 117, No. 6, pp. 24–30 (June 1994).

increase in the number of married mothers with children under 18 who worked year-round full time. In 1970, 16.4% did, whereas by 1992 it had more than doubled to 36.8%.

Although women with children under age 6 do have a lower labor force participation rate than those with children 6–17, it is significant that the gains have been even more rapid. For instance, in 1970 only 9.6% of married mothers with children under 6 worked year-round full time, but by 1992 that had more than tripled to 30.6%.

At the end of 1992, 67.1% of nearly 12 million married women with children under 6 were in the labor force indicating a need for a substantial amount of child care. Likewise, 78.4% of almost 13 million married mothers with school age children were in the labor force, a figure which indicates a need for after-school and school vacation care.

2.3. Government Policies on Child Care

At the outset, it should be noted that in the United States education is primarily the responsibility of the fifty states. The federal government can support education through a variety of means, most notably federal funding. It also means that government policy is not monolithic as there are fifty state governments plus the federal government.

In the United States, children typically enter school at age 5 or 6. Most children start first grade at age 6. Most children stay in school until high school graduation, which occurs around age 17–18. In most school districts, the school day is approximately 8:30 am – 3 pm. Although the school year varies by state, the school year typically begins in early September and runs until the latter part of June.

In many school districts, it has been customary to provide a phased in introduction to school prior to first grade. This is often called 'kindergarten' and is usually designed for children age 5. If kindergarten is offered by the local public (state) school, it is typically free of charge. Kindergarten may be full day or half day (usually mornings). In the last twenty years, the increasing number of working mothers has meant that school districts have been pressured to offer kindergarten and to have full day kindergartens. Consequently, the number of school districts offering full day kindergartens has increased greatly but it is by no means universal.

The United States has never had a policy of government funding of pre-school or nursery school centers, along the lines found in France or the Scandanavian countries. The main exception has been for low income children. Under President Johnson's Great Society initiative, 'Get Set' and 'Head Start' centers were established for low income children. This program was never funded sufficiently to cover all low income children who qualified for the program, and in fact, funding declined very substantially during the 1980s for this program.

The bulk of day care centers and pre-schools are privately operated, some for profit and some on a non-profit basis. As for private day care centers, nursery schools and pre-schools, there are no federal standards, nor any federal licensing of day care workers or pre-school teachers. Regulation by the states varies greatly. Because day care center costs and pre-school tuition are paid for by parents, the actual conditions in day care centers and pre-schools varies greatly. As might be expected, upper middle class parents can afford to pay significantly more per week for child care than working class parents and conditions in day care centers reflect this.

2.4. Business Response to Work-Family Pressures

The increasing number of working women with children has compelled employers to grapple with the sometimes conflicting demands of work and family life. From a topic that was rarely mentioned twenty years ago, work-family life is now on the agenda of most human resource management conferences.[8] The business imperative that has generated this discussion is the need to retain valued employees.

In contrast to some other countries, women in the United States are equally as well educated as men.[9] Well educated women tend to delay childbearing. As a result, when a college educated female becomes pregnant with her first child, she typically has been with the company for five – seven years. The employer has invested significantly in that employee's human capital and does not want to lose the employee if some arrangement can be worked out with the employee. Consequently, despite the lack of any legal mandates before 1993, employers did offer maternity leave (typically 6–8 weeks under short-term disability coverage). Employers did permit new mothers to tack on vacation leave and accumulated leave time on to the maternity leave. As a result, it was not uncommon for better educated women, working year round full time, to be able to take off three or four months when at the time of the baby's birth. Many employers also voluntarily offered unpaid leave, a phased-in return to work, reduced working hours, flex time and job sharing. The use of these policies, which has been increasing over time, are spreading more rapidly now that the Family and Medical Leave Act has taken effect.

Some large firms, and firms where employees bill by the hour (such as law firms and accounting firms) have begun to contract with services that provide 'sick child care.' For instance, a young child with a bad cold who cannot go to day care can be dropped off by his parent at the sick child drop-in center. Some companies have set up their own day care center in or near the company's premises. This has not proved practical for many companies. As a result, it is more common for companies to assist employees with finding day care, and with subsidizing the cost of the day care offered by a private center.

Except for maternity leave, all the other policies mentioned above are still entirely voluntary. Magazine articles and the publications of human resource management associations mention them routinely. Accurate data based on a national survey is lacking, and even what exists tends to omit those companies employing less than 100 (and thus omit the bulk of female employment).

This reporter can only say, both from anecdotal evidence and personal observation, that it is routine for companies to make some accommodation of employees' needs. The accommodation is so routine that it is often not recorded. For instance, the exact starting time of work for a female office worker may reflect her need to drop her child off at school or the day care center but only she and her supervisor know the reason for the exact starting time. The scheduling of the employee's vacation time may also relate to her child's schedule. Similarly, only the immediate su-

8. Here it should be noted that the leading practitioner association, the Society for Human Resource Management, with 57,000 members is 56% female.

9. Historically, women may have had lower educational levels, but at the present time a higher percentage of girls graduate high school than boys because boys have a significantly higher drop out rate. Of students enrolled in colleges and universities, more than 50% are female. This may reflect the fact that some well paying fields that do not require a college education (such as the skilled trades) are traditionally male.

pervisor or co-workers may know if a parent brings a child into the office for a day because the child's school is closed and there is no alternative care arrangement.

One change in policy that has occurred in the last twenty years has certainly been accelerated by the needs of working parents. In the 1960s, it was common for most companies to offer vacation days (typically based on length of service) and holidays (offered to all). Holidays were designated; e.g., New Year's Day, Thanksgiving Day. In the past twenty years, the concept of 'personal days' has emerged. For instance, a company may stipulate that there are seven holidays and three personal days. An employee may use personal days for any reason whatsoever. For example, a young, unmarried employee might take off on his birthday. In contrast, a working mother might use a personal day when her child is home sick. A more recent accommodation to employees' needs has been the willingness of some employers to permit employees to use their sick days in order to care for sick children.

Despite the willingness of employers' to make some accommodation for employees' needs, there is growing awareness that there is an inadequate supply of quality care at affordable prices for young children. There is awareness that the schedules of day care centers, pre-schools, schools, and summer camps do not always mesh well with the work schedules of the child's parents.

2.5. Government Leave Mandates

After several vetoes during the adminstrations of Presidents Reagan and Bush, Congress passed the Family and Medical Leave Act of 1993 (FMLA), signed into law by President Clinton. This law took effect in August 1993. Because this statute is so recent, there is no body of case law. This report will confine itself to explaining the statute's provisions.

The FMLA covers all public sector employers. It also covers all private sector employers who in the current or preceding calendar year have employed 50 or more employees in 20 or more workweeks.

To be eligible for benefits under the FMLA, an employee must work for a covered employer, must have worked for the employer for a total of at least one year, and must have worked at least 1250 hours over the previous year. Thus, an employee who works twenty hours per week year round will be covered.

A covered employer must grant an eligible employee up to a total of 12 work weeks of unpaid leave during any 12-month period for one or more of the following reasons:

- upon the birth of a child or upon the placement of a child for adoption or foster care;
- to care for an immediate family member (spouse, child, or parent) with a serious health condition;
- to take medical leave when the employee is unable to work because of a serious health condition.[10]

A 'serious health condition' is one the requires an overnight hospital (or other residential medical care facility) stay, or any period of incapacity requiring absence of more than three calendar days from work, school or regular daily activities and that also involves continuing treatment by a health care provider.

---

10. Until the passage of this statute, the United States did not oblige employers to grant sick leave, paid or unpaid, of any duration. Larger employers typically granted paid sick leave but among medium-sized and small employers the situation varied greatly.

Although the FMLA is much broader than a maternity leave act, it does serve to guarantee new mothers an unpaid maternity leave of twelve weeks. For Americans, the FMLA adopts a 'unisex' approach; that is, both of the baby's parents can take a leave to care for the baby.[11] By the standards of some countries, a twelve week new parent leave may seem short. For Americans, it is a very substantial legal guarantee. Likewise, the legal guarantee of leave to time to care for an immediate family member with a serious health condition, or to take time off for the employee's own medical care is a very significant advance in employment protection.

3. BALANCING WORK AND FAMILY LIFE

The 1993 FMLA introduces an entirely new concept for Americans; namely, that employees need not risk their jobs to take time off to care for an infant or a family member with a serious health condition. While some companies, particularly larger companies, had in fact followed an approach that attempted to accommodate employees with such needs, there was no legal guarantee. There is still, however, difficulty in reconciling the demands of work with the demands of ongoing, long term care giving.

3.1. Child Care

When a child is under six, full time work by both parents presents the most challenging situation. Very young children periodically are mildly ill, perhaps with a bad cold or ear infection. The baby sitter may take off a day sick or the day care center may be closed on a work day. In all these situations, one parent must take off from work to care for the child.

Aside from the problems mentioned above, there are other difficulties. Given the difficulty of finding good child care and the expense of such care, it is not surprising that parents resort to various stratagems to avoid paying for full-time day child care. Many women stop working full time when their children are young. Many working mothers work shift work and arrange their shifts so that the father can be at home with the child while the mother is at work. In 1991, the primary child care arrangements used by working mothers[12] of children under five were as follows: 36% of children were cared for in their own homes (mainly by their fathers), 31% were cared for in another home (usually by someone not related to the child), and 23% were in organized child care facilities (mostly those children aged 3–5).

Once children are of school age, care becomes easier. Data reveals that many women switch from part time back to full time work. Even so, problems remain. After school programs are becoming more common but are not universal. Many working parents report anxiety about their children being home alone until one parent arrives home from work. This phenomenon, called 'the latchkey child,' is increasing. The use of this form of self care increases with age. Less than 5% of children

11. When both parents work for the same company, they are entitled to twelve weeks' total leave time to care for the infant. The two parents can decide whether and how each parent will claim leave.

12. For one of the most comprehensive surveys on this subject, *see* Lynee M. Casper, Mary Hawkins and Martin O'Connell, 'Who's Minding the Kids?, Child Care Arrangements: Fall' 1991, U.S. Department of Commerce, Bureau of the Census, *Current Population Reports p. 70–36* (May 1994).

under 10 are reported to be home alone, whereas 20% of children age 14 are home alone after school.

3.2. Elder Care

The increase in the percentage of women aged 44–54 who are in the labor force and the aging of the American population taken together would indicate that the problem of elder care is a serious one in the United States. In addition, compared to many other societies, America is relatively mobile. Thus, a middle-aged employee often does not live near an aged parent. Becuase of this, simple but necessary chores, such as buying groceries or cleaning house, become heavy burdens on the employed child.

Employer responses to the elder care demands placed on employees are not well developed. In part this results from the fact that elder care is more challenging than child care. Elder care burdens usually increase over time (unlike child care burdens which lessen over time). Elder care burdens, unlike child care, often fluctuate unpredictably. For instance, an aged parent may be hospitalized for a stroke or a heart attack. The child may be required to be at a hospital for days. The aged parent may be switched to a rehabilitation facility or a nursing home. The child may be required only to visit, or there may be heavier burdens (such as transporting the parent from home to the rehabilitation facility). The duties that are performed for aged persons in some countries by home health visitors (such as cleaning, bathing, feeding) who are paid through a government health insurance program must be paid for privately in the United States. As this is very costly, there is a strong financial need for the child to perform such duties outside of work time.

An authoritative, comprehensive study of the elder care needs of employed persons does not exist. Much of what is written on this topic states anecdotal evidence, or is based on small surveys. It has been estimated that about 10–15% of employees provide care to an elderly relative, with the typical care giver a married 45 year old woman who is employed full time.[13] Some estimate that as many as one-third of the employed care givers live more than 100 miles from the elderly person needing care. All employers questioned in surveys report that elder care demands on employees result in higher absenteeism and in a general loss of productivity due to stress.

The 1990 census revealed that 31.1 million persons, or 12.5% of the population, were over age 65.[14] Among the elderly, 18 million were aged 65–74; 10 million were aged 75–84; and 3 million were 85 or older. The elderly population increased by 22% in the 1980s. In contrast, between 1990 and 2010, the growth of the older population will not be dramatic, because of the low birth rates in the 1930s. From 2010 to 2030, hoever, the elderly population will grow by about 73% while the population under age 65 will probably decrease by about 3%.[15]

The needs of the elderly vary by age. By age 85, nearly 25% live in nursing homes. Of those over 85 who are not institutionalized, 45% need personal assistance with everyday activities. Especially needy are elderly women because they are more

---

13. Nancy Nager and Terence McGowan, 'Elder Care: The Employee Benefit of the 1990s', *Compensation and Benefits Management*, pp. 44–48 (Spring 1994).
14. The data on the elderly is extracted from Cynthia M. Taeuber, 'Sixty-Five Plus in America', U.S. Department of Commerce, Bureau of the Census, *Current Population Reports, pp. 23–178*, (August 1992).
15. This trend results from the huge jump in fertility in the period 1946–1960. This bulge in the population is called the 'baby boom.'

likely than elderly men to have long-term, chronic disabling diseases. The over-85 group, then, represents the most needy group among the elderly. It is this group that demands the most care, and this group will double in size between 1990 and 2010 (from 3.1 million to an estimated 6.2 million).

3.2.1. Government and Employer Elder Care Policies

There are no laws mandating that a worker be given time off to care for the elderly except for the Family and Medical Leave Act. Under the FMLA, an eligible employee does have a right to 12 weeks of unpaid leave each year to care for an immediate family member who has a serious health condition. Thus, if an employee's father has a stroke, is hospitalized, and then spends a period in a skilled nursing home, the employee could take leave. If, however, the employee's 87 year old mother lives alone and needs frequent in daily activities (shopping, going to doctor's appointments, cleaning), there is no guaranteed leave. The FMLA has been in effect only since August 1993, and cases have not yet illuminated the dimensions of the leave guarantee as applied to the elderly.

Within the past decade, a major change has occurred in employer attitudes. Prior to the 1980, 'elder care' was an unknown term. More importantly, most company executives did not even recognize it as a need. Today, all medium and large companies recognize that employees are burdened by elder care needs. Many are responding by voluntarily granting time off. Nonetheless, the dimensions of the problem suggest that better solutions must be developed.

www.ingramcontent.com/pod-product-compliance
Lightning Source LLC
Chambersburg PA
CBHW071350230926
51846CB00002B/494

* 9 7 8 9 0 4 1 1 0 0 6 4 1 *